SEX,
ECONOMY,
FREEDOM
&
COMMUNITY

ALSO BY WENDELL BERRY

FICTION

Fidelity
The Discovery of Kentucky
The Memory of Old Jack
Nathan Coulter
A Place on Earth
Remembering
The Wild Birds

POETRY

Clearing
Collected Poems: 1957–1982
The Country of Marriage
Farming: A Hand Book
Openings
A Part
Sabbaths
Sayings and Doings
Traveling at Home
The Wheel

ESSAYS

A Continuous Harmony
The Gift of Good Land
Harland Hubbard: Life and Work
The Hidden Wound
Home Economics
Recollected Essays: 1965–1980
Standing by Words
The Unforeseen Wilderness
The Unsettling of America
What Are People For?

SEX, ECONOMY, FREEDOM & COMMUNITY

E I G H T   E S S A Y S

WENDELL BERRY

PANTHEON BOOKS

NEW YORK AND SAN FRANCISCO

Copyright © 1992, 1993 by Wendell Berry

I am grateful to the Louisville Community Foundation, which printed parts I and II of "Sex, Economy, Freedom, and Community" as a pamphlet, and also to the editors of the following periodicals, in whose pages some of the other essays in the book were previously printed: *The Louisville Courier-Journal*, *The Atlantic Monthly*, *The Progressive*, *Journal of the Soil and Water Conservation Society*, *Wild Earth*, *Amicus Journal*, *The Land Report*, *Appalachia*, *Northern Forest Forum*.

Library of Congress Cataloging-in-Publication Data
Berry, Wendell, 1934—
     Sex, economy, freedom & community : eight essays / Wendell Berry.
          p.   cm.
     Includes bibliographical references
     ISBN 0-679-42394-X
     1. United States—Social conditions.   2. Social problems.
3. Community.   I. Title.
HN59.2.B47   1993
306'.0973—dc20   93-769

Book design by Maura Fadden Rosenthal

Manufactured in the United States of America
First Edition
9   8   7   6   5   4   3   2   1

I dedicate this book to the memory of Harry M. Caudill and Edward Abbey, great defenders of their homelands, and of Tom Marsh, who taught that the useful could and should be beautiful.

CONTENTS

PREFACE

THE JOY OF SALES RESISTANCE   xi

CHAPTER ONE

CONSERVATION AND LOCAL ECONOMY   3

CHAPTER TWO

OUT OF YOUR CAR, OFF YOUR HORSE   19

CHAPTER THREE

CONSERVATION IS GOOD WORK   27

CHAPTER FOUR

A BAD BIG IDEA   45

CHAPTER FIVE

THE PROBLEM OF TOBACCO   53

CHAPTER SIX

PEACEABLENESS TOWARD ENEMIES   69

CHAPTER SEVEN

CHRISTIANITY AND THE SURVIVAL OF CREATION   93

CHAPTER EIGHT

SEX, ECONOMY, FREEDOM, AND COMMUNITY   117

NOTES   175

For help with various parts of this book or all of it, I thank Tanya Berry, John M. Berry, Jr., Ross Feld, Philip Sherrard, Joseph Bryant, Hal Hamilton, Mark Ritchie, John Daniel, Nancy Palmer Jones, and the entire staff of the West Coast office of Pantheon Books.

PREFACE: THE JOY
OF SALES RESISTANCE

Dear Reader,

This is a book about sales resistance. We live in a time when technologies and ideas (often the same thing) are adopted in response not to need but to advertising, salesmanship, and fashion. Salesmen and saleswomen now hover about us as persistently as angels, intent on "doing us good" according to instructions set forth by persons educated at great public expense in the arts of greed and prevarication. These salespeople are now with most of us, apparently, even in our dreams.

The first duty of writers who wish to be of any use even to themselves is to resist the language, the ideas, and the categories of this ubiquitous sales talk, no matter from whose mouth it issues. But, then, this is also the first duty of everybody else. Nobody who is awake accepts the favors of these hawkers of guaranteed satisfactions, these escape artists, these institutional and commercial fanatics, whether politically correct or politically incorrect. Nobody who understands the history of justice or of the imagination (largely the same history) wants to be treated as a member of a category.

I am more and more impressed by the generality of the assumption that human lives are properly to be invented by an academic-corporate-governmental elite and then either sold to their passive and choiceless recipients or doled out to them in the manner of welfare payments. Any necessary thinking—so the assumption goes—will be done by certified smart people in offices, laboratories, boardrooms, and other high places and then will be handed down to supposedly unsmart people in low places—who will also be expected to do whatever actual work cannot be done cheaper by machines.

Such a society, whose members are expected to think and do and provide nothing for themselves, will necessarily give a high place to salesmanship. For such a society cannot help but encourage the growth of a kind of priesthood of men and women who know exactly what you need and who just happen to have it for you, attractively packaged and at a price no competitor can beat. If you wish to be among the beautiful, then you must buy the right fashions (there are no cheap fashions) and the right automobile (not cheap either). If you want to be counted as one of the intelligent, then you must shop for the right education (not cheap but also not difficult).

Actually, as we know, the new commercial education is fun for everybody. All you have to do in order to have or to provide such an education is to pay your money (in advance) and master a few simple truths:

  1. Educated people are more valuable than other people because education is a value-adding industry.

II. Educated people are better than other people because education improves people and makes them good.

III. The purpose of education is to make people able to earn more and more money.

IV. The place where education is to be used is called "your career."

V. Anything that cannot be weighed, measured, or counted does not exist.

VI. The so-called humanities probably do not exist. But if they do, they are useless. But whether they exist or not or are useful or not, they can sometimes be made to support a career.

VII. Literacy does not involve knowing the meanings of words, or learning grammar, or reading books.

VIII. The sign of exceptionally smart people is that they speak a language that is intelligible only to other people in their "field" or only to themselves. This is very impressive and is known as "professionalism."

IX. The smartest and most educated people are the scientists, for they have already found solutions to all our problems and will soon find solutions to all the problems resulting from their solutions to all the problems we used to have.

X. The mark of a good teacher is that he or she spends most of his or her time doing research and writes many books and articles.

xi. The mark of a good researcher is the same as that of a good teacher.

xii. A great university has many computers, a lot of government and corporation research contracts, a winning team, and more administrators than teachers.

xiii. Computers make people even better and smarter than they were made by previous thingamabobs. Or if some people prove incorrigibly wicked or stupid or both, computers will at least speed them up.

xiv. The main thing is, don't let education get in the way of being nice to children. Children are our Future. Spend plenty of money on them but don't stay home with them and get in their way. Don't give them work to do; they are smart and can think up things to do on their own. Don't teach them any of that awful, stultifying, repressive, old-fashioned morality. Provide plenty of TV, microwave dinners, day care, computers, computer games, cars. For all this, they will love and respect us and be glad to grow up and pay our debts.

xv. A good school is a big school.

xvi. Disarm the children before you let them in.

Of course, education is for the Future, and the Future is one of our better-packaged items and attracts many buyers. (The past, on the other hand, is hard to sell; it is, after all, past.) The Future is where we'll all be fulfilled, happy, healthy, and perhaps will live and consume forever. It may have some bad things in it, like storms or floods or earthquakes or plagues or volcanic eruptions or stray meteors, but soon we will learn to predict and prevent such things before they happen. In the Future, many scientists will be employed in figuring out how to prevent the unpredictable consequences of the remaining unpreventable bad things. There will always be work for scientists.

The Future, as everybody knows, is a subject of extreme importance to politicians, and we have several political packages that are almost irresistible—expensive, of course, but rare:

1. **Tolerance and Multiculturalism.** Quit talking bad about women, homosexuals, and preferred social minorities, and you can say anything you want about people who haven't been to college, manual workers, country people, peasants, religious people, unmodern people, old people, and so on. Tolerant and multicultural persons hyphenate their land of origin and their nationality. I, for example, am a Kentuckian-American.

2. **Preservation of Human Resources.** Despite world-record advances in automation, robotification, and other "labor-saving" technologies, it is assumeed that almost every human being may, at least in the Future, turn out to be useful for something, just like the members of other endangered species. Sometimes, after all, the Economy still requires a "human component." At such times, human resources are called "human components" and are highly esteemed in that capacity as long as their usefulness lasts. Therefore, don't quit taking care of human resources yet. See that the schools are run as ideal orphanages or as ideal jails. Provide preschool and pre-preschool. Also postschool. Keep the children in institutions and away from home as much as possible—remember that their parents

wanted children only because other people have them, and are much too busy to raise them. Only the government cares. Move the children around a lot while they're young, for this provides many opportunities for socialization. Show them a lot of TV, for TV is educational. Teach them about computers, for computers still require a "human component." Teach them the three S's: Sex can be Scientific and Safe. When the children grow up, try to keep them busy. Try to see that they become addicted only to legal substances. That's about it.

3. **Reducing the Government.** The government should only be big enough to annihilate any country and (if necessary) every country, to spy on its citizens and on other governments, to keep big secrets, and to see to the health and happiness of large corporations. A government thus reduced will be almost too small to notice and will require almost no taxes and spend almost no money.

4. **The Free Market.** The free market sees to it that everything ends up in the right place—that is, it makes sure that only the worthy get rich. All millionaires and billionaires have worked hard for their money, and they deserve the rewards of their work. They need all the help they can get from the government and the universities. Having money stimulates the rich to further economic activity that ultimately benefits the rest of us. Needing money stimulates the rest of us to further economic activity that ultimately benefits the rich. The cardinal principle of the free market is unrestrained competition, which is a kind of tournament that will decide which is the world's champion corporation. Ultimately, thanks to this principle, there will be only one

corporation, which will be wonderfully simplifying. After that, we will rest in peace.

5. **Unlimited Economic Growth.** This is the pet idea of the Party of Hardheaded Realists. That unlimited economic growth can be accomplished within limited space, with limited materials and limited intelligence, only shows the unlimited courage and self-confidence of these Great Minds. That unlimited economic growth implies unlimited consumption, which in turn implies unlimited pride, covetousness, lust, anger, gluttony, envy, and sloth, only makes the prospect even more unlimited.

Or, finally, we might consider the package known as:

6. **The Food System,** which is one of my favorites. The Food System is firmly grounded on the following principles:

i. Food is important mainly as an article of international trade.

ii. It doesn't matter what happens to farmers.

iii. It doesn't matter what happens to the land.

iv. Agriculture has nothing to do with "the environment."

v. There will always be plenty of food, for if farmers don't grow it from the soil, then scientists will invent it.

vi. There is no connection between food and health. People are fed by the food industry, which pays no attention to health, and are healed by the health industry, which pays no attention to food.

vii. It follows that there is no connection between healing and health. Hospitals customarily feed their patients poor-quality, awful-tasting, factory-made expensive food and keep them awake all night with various expensive attentions. There *is* a connection between money and health.

In this Christmassy atmosphere, an essayist must be aware of the danger of becoming just one more in this mob of drummers. He (as a matter of syntactical convenience, I am speaking only of men essayists) had better understand with some care what it is that he has to sell, what he has to give away, and certainly also what he may have that nobody else will want.

I do have an interest in this book, which is for sale. (If you have bought it, dear reader, I thank you. If you have borrowed it, I honor your frugality. If you have stolen it, may it add to your confusion.) Most of the sale price pays the publisher for paper, ink, and other materials, for editorial advice, copyediting, design, advertising (I hope), and marketing. I get between 10 and 15 percent (depending on sales) for arranging the words on the pages.

As I understand it, I am being paid only for my work in arranging the words; my property is that arrangement. The thoughts in this book, on the contrary, are not mine. They came freely to me, and I give them freely away. I have no "intellectual property," and I think that all claimants to such property are thieves.

———

I am, I acknowledge, a white Protestant heterosexual man, and can only offer myself as such. I take no particular pride in my membership in this unfashionable group, nor do I consider myself in any way its spokesman. I do, however, ask you to note, dear reader, that this membership confers on me a certain usefulness in that it leaves me with no excuses and nobody to blame for my faults except myself. In fact, I am only grateful to my parents, my family, and my friends, who have done their best to make me better than I am. On my more charitable days, I am grateful even to my enemies, who have sharpened my mind and who have done me the service of being, as a rule, wronger than I am.

I am well aware that you cannot give your thoughts to someone who will not take them, and I am prepared for that. I would like to be agreed with, of course, but the rules of publication require me to be willing also to be disagreed with, to be ignored, and even to be disliked. Those who are moved by this book to disagreement or dislike will take discomfort, I hope, from hearing that some of my readers treat me kindly.

Kindness from readers is something that no essayist (and no writer of any other kind) has a right to expect. The kindness I have received from readers I count as the only profit from my work that is entirely net. I am always grateful for it and often am deeply moved by it.

But kindness is not—is never—the same as complete agreement. An essayist not only has no right to expect complete agreement but has a certain responsibility to ward it off. If you tell me, dear reader, that you agree with me completely, then I must suspect one or both of us of dishonesty. I must reserve the right, after all, to disagree with myself.

But however much I may change my mind, I will

never agree with those saleswomen and salesmen who suggest that if I will only do as they say, all will be fine. All, dear reader, is not going to be fine. Even if we all agreed with all the saints and prophets, all would not be fine. For we would still be mortal, partial, suffering poor creatures, not very intelligent and never the authors of our best hope.

Yours sincerely,
Wendell Berry

P.S. Last summer, for example, I read a newspaper article* announcing, in the awestricken voice of the science journalist, "a new generation of technological inventions—most of them involving some variation on the home computer." The two inventions specifically described in the article were electronic newspapers and something called "hypertext."

The benefits of the electronic newspaper apparently all have to do with convenience: "These screens will display a front page with an index. The user can tap a pen to the screen to call up a story, flip a page, turn a still photograph into a TV news scene, or even make a dinner or theatre reservation from an ad."

Hypertext "makes it possible to create all sorts of linkages and short circuits within a text." And this "is extremely useful in organizing technical material so that the reader can efficiently select which parts of a text to read." The reason for this, according to a "consultant," is that "usually you don't want to read everything— you only want to read what you don't know." Hypertext

---

* "What Is Going to Become of the Written Word?" by Walter Truett Anderson (Pacific News Service), *The Mountain Eagle* (Whitesburg, KY), July 22, 1992, 4 and 8.

"is reader-friendly and makes it easy to chart a path to the desired parts."

Thanks also to this invention, "creative-writing professors are teaching courses about how to write hypertext novels that literally go in all directions." These novels are "interactive":

> In reading a hypertext novel you may follow the point of view of a chosen character, or you may choose the outcome you like best, or you may wander off into subtleties beyond anything James Joyce could have imagined. The possibilities—and the stories—may be endless.
>
> This opens up new realms of choice and creativity. In some ways it frees the reader from being merely a passive receptacle of the author's genius (or lack of same).

Dear reader, I hope you will understand at least somewhat the disgust, the contempt, and the joy with which I have received this news.

It disgusts me because I know there is no need for such products, which will put a lot of money into the pockets of people who don't care how they earn it and will bring another downward turn in the effort of gullible people to become better and smarter by way of machinery. This is a perfect example of modern salesmanship and modern technology—yet another way to make people pay dearly for what they already have (the ability to turn the pages of a newspaper or respond to an ad; the ability to read and write, to choose what to read, and to read "actively").

I read about these things with contempt because of the nonsense and the falsehood involved. For example, no real comparison is made in this article between paper newspapers and electronic ones. The stated difference is simply that one is newer and somehow easier than the other. And what exactly is implied by the use of a machine that makes it possible to read only "what you don't know"? Is this perhaps what we call "skimming"? But how do you know, without reading or at least skimming, whether you know or do not know what is in a text? And what of the pleasure of reading again what you already know? The assumption here is that reading is an ordeal, of which the less said the better. And don't we remember that television was once expected to produce a new era of general enlightenment? And now will we believe that the electronically stupefied will turn from their soap operas to "hypertext" and indulge themselves in "subtleties and complexities" beyond the powers of James Joyce? And are we to suppose that readers of, say, James Joyce have hitherto been mere passive receptacles of his genius? And haven't we known all along that the stories are endless?

My joy comes from my instantaneous knowledge that I am not going to buy either piece of equipment. When the inevitable saleswoman comes to tell me that I cannot be up-to-date, or intelligent, or creative, or handsome, or young, or eligible for the sexual favors of so fair a creature as herself unless I buy these products, dear reader, I am not going to do it.

Somewhere is better than anywhere.
　　　　—Flannery O'Connor

SEX,
ECONOMY,
FREEDOM
&
COMMUNITY

CONSERVATION AND LOCAL ECONOMY

In our relation to the land, we are ruled by a number of terms and limits set not by anyone's preference but by nature and by human nature:

I. Land that is used will be ruined unless it is properly cared for.

II. Land cannot be properly cared for by people who do not know it intimately, who do not know how to care for it, who are not strongly motivated to care for it, and who cannot afford to care for it.

III. People cannot be adequately motivated to care for land by general principles or by incentives that are merely economic—that is, they won't care for it merely because they think they should or merely because somebody pays them.

IV. People are motivated to care for land to the extent that their interest in it is direct, dependable, and permanent.

v. They will be motivated to care for the land if they can reasonably expect to live on it as long as they live. They will be more strongly motivated if they can reasonably expect that their children and grandchildren will live on it as long as they live. In other words, there must be a mutuality of belonging: they must feel that the land belongs to them, that they belong to it, and that this belonging is a settled and unthreatened fact.

vi. But such belonging must be appropriately limited. This is the indispensable qualification of the idea of land ownership. It is well understood that ownership is an incentive to care. But there is a limit to how much land can be owned before an owner is unable to take proper care of it. The need for attention increases with the intensity of use. But the *quality* of attention decreases as acreage increases.

vii. A nation will destroy its land and therefore itself if it does not foster in every possible way the sort of thrifty, prosperous, permanent rural households and communities that have the desire, the skills, and the means to care properly for the land they are using.

In an age notoriously impatient of restraints, such a list of rules will hardly be welcome, but that these *are* the rules of land use I have no doubt. I am convinced of their authenticity both by common wisdom and by my own experience and observation. The rules exist; the penalties for breaking them are obvious and severe; the failure of land stewardship in this country is the result of a general disregard for all of them.

As proof of this failure, there is no need to recite again the statistics of land ruination. The gullies and other damages are there to be seen. Very little of our land that is being used—for logging, mining, or farming—is being well used. Much of our land has never been well used. Those of us who know what we are looking at know that this is true. And after observing the worsening condition of our land, we have only to raise our eyes a little to see the worsening condition of those who are using the land and who are entrusted with its care. We must accept as a fact that by now, our country (as opposed to our nation) is characteristically in decline. War, depression, inflation, usury, the attitudes of the industrial economy, social and educational fashions—all have taken their toll. For a long time, the news from everywhere in rural America has been almost unrelievedly bad: bankruptcy, foreclosure, depression, suicide, the departure of the young, the loneliness of the old, soil loss, soil degradation, chemical pollution, the loss of genetic and specific diversity, the extinction or threatened extinction of species, the depletion of aquifers, stream degradation, the loss of wilderness, strip mining, clear-cutting, population loss, the loss of supporting economies, the deaths of towns. Rural American communities, economies, and ways of life that in 1945 were thriving and, though imperfect, full of promise for an authentic human settlement of our land are now as effectively destroyed as the Jewish communities of Poland; the means of destruction were not so blatantly evil, but they have proved just as thorough.

The news of rural decline and devastation has been accompanied, to be sure, by a chorus of professional, institutional, and governmental optimists, who continue to insist that all is well, that we are making things worse only as a way of making things better, that farmers who failed are merely "inefficient producers" for whose failure the country is better off, that money and technology will fill the gaps, that government will fill the gaps, that science will soon free us from our regrettable dependence on the soil. We have heard that it is good business and good labor economics to destroy the last remnants of American wilderness. We have heard that the rural population is actually growing because city people are moving to the country and commuters are replacing farmers. We have heard that the rural economy can be repaired by moving the urban economy out into the country and by replacing rural work with work in factories and offices. And all the while the real conditions of the rural land and the rural people have been getting worse.

Of the general condition of the American countryside, my own community will serve well enough as an example. The town of Port Royal, Kentucky, has a population of about one hundred people. The town came into existence as a trading center, serving the farms in a few square miles of hilly country on the west side of the Kentucky River. It has never been much bigger than it is now. But whereas now it is held together by habit or convenience, once it was held together by a complex local economy. In my mother's childhood, in the years before World War I, there were sixteen business and professional enterprises in the town, all serving the town and the surrounding farms. By the time of my own childhood, in the years before World War II, the number had been reduced to twelve, but the town and its tributary landscape were still alive as a community and as an economy. Now, counting the post office, the town has five enterprises, one of which does not serve the local community. There is now no market for farm produce in the town or within forty miles. We no longer have a garage or repair shop of any kind. We have had no doctor for forty years and no school for thirty. Now, as a local economy and therefore as a community, Port Royal is dying.

What does the death of a community, a local economy, cost its members? And what does it cost the country? So far as I know, we have no economists who are interested in such costs. Nevertheless, when you must drive ten or twenty or more miles to reach a doctor or a school or a mechanic or to find parts for farm machinery, the costs exist, and they are increasing. As they increase, they make the economy of every farm and household less tenable.

As people leave the community or, remaining in the place, drop out of the local economy, as the urban-industrial economy more and more usurps the local economy, as the scale and speed of work increase, care declines. As care declines, the natural supports of the human economy and community also decline, for whatever is used, is used destructively.

We in Port Royal are part of an agricultural region surrounded by cities that import much of their food from distant places. Though we urgently need crops that can be substituted for tobacco, we produce practically no vegetables or other foods for consumption in our region. Having no local food economy, we produce a less and less diverse food supply for the general market. This condition implies and virtually requires the abuse of our land and our people, and they are abused.

We are also part of a region that is abundantly and diversely forested, and we have no forest economy. We have no local wood products industry. This makes it

almost certain that our woodlands and their owners will
be abused, and they are abused.

We provide, moreover, a great deal of recreation
for our urban neighbors—hunting, fishing, boating, and
the like—and we have the capacity to provide more.
But for this we receive little or nothing, and sometimes
we suffer damage.

In our region, furthermore, there has been no public
effort to preserve the least scrap of land in its pristine
condition. And the last decade or so of agricultural
depression has caused much logging of the few stands
of mature forest in private hands. Now, if we want our
descendants to know what the original forest was like
—that is, to know the original nature of our land—we
must start from scratch and grow the necessary examples over the next two or three hundred years.

My part of rural America is, in short, a colony, like
every other part of rural America. Almost the whole
landscape of this country—from the exhausted cotton
fields of the plantation South to the eroding wheatlands
of the Palouse, from the strip mines of Appalachia to
the clear-cuts of the Pacific slope—is in the power of
an absentee economy, once national and now increasingly international, that is without limit in its greed and
without mercy in its exploitation of land and people.
Between the prosperity of this vast centralizing economy and the prosperity of any local economy or locality,
there is now a radical disconnection. The accounting
that measures the wealth of corporations, great banks,
and national treasuries takes no measure of the civic or
economic or natural health of places like Port Royal,
Kentucky; Harpster, Ohio; Indianola, Iowa; Matfield
Green, Kansas; Wolf Hole, Arizona; or Nevada City,
California—and it does not intend to do so.

In 1912, according to William Allen White, "the county in the United States with the largest assessed valuation was Marion County, Kansas. . . . Marion County happened to have a larger per capita of bank deposits than any other American county. . . . Yet no man in Marion County was rated as a millionaire, but the jails and poorhouses were practically empty. The great per capita of wealth was actually distributed among the people who earned it." This, of course, is the realization of that dream that is sometimes called Jeffersonian but is really the dream of the economically oppressed throughout human history. And because this was a rural county, White was not talking just about bank accounts; he was talking about real capital—usable property. That era and that dream are now long past. Now the national economy, which is increasingly a global economy, no longer prospers by the prosperity of the land and people but by their exploitation.

The Civil War made America safe for the moguls of the railroads and of the mineral and timber industries who wanted to be free to exploit the countryside. The work of these industries and their successors is now almost complete. They have dispossessed, disinherited, and moved into the urban economy almost the entire citizenry; they have defaced and plundered the coun‑ tryside. And now this great corporate enterprise, thoroughly uprooted and internationalized, is moving toward the exploitation of the whole world under the shibboleths of "globalization," "free trade," and "new world order." The proposed revisions in the General Agreement on Tariffs and Trade are intended solely to further this exploitation. The aim is simply and unabashedly to bring every scrap of productive land and every worker on the planet under corporate control.

The voices of the countryside, the voices appealing for respect for the land and for rural community, have simply not been heard in the centers of wealth, power, and knowledge. The centers have decreed that the voice of the countryside shall be that of Snuffy Smith or L'il Abner, and only that voice have they been willing to hear.

"The business of America is business," a prophet of our era too correctly said. Two corollaries are clearly implied: that the business of the American government is to serve, protect, and defend business; and that the business of the American people is to serve the government, which means to serve business. The costs of this state of things are incalculable. To start with, people in great numbers—because of their perception that the government serves not the country or the people but the corporate economy—do not vote. Our leaders, therefore, are now in the curious—and hardly legitimate—position of asking a very substantial number of people to cheer for, pay for, and perhaps die for a government that they have not voted for.

But when the interests of local communities and economies are relentlessly subordinated to the interests of "business," then two further catastrophes inevitably result. First, the people are increasingly estranged from the native wealth, health, knowledge, and pleasure of their country. And, second, the country itself is destroyed.

It is not possible to look at the present condition of our land and people and find support for optimism. We must not fool ourselves. It is altogether conceivable that we may go right along with this business of "business," with our curious religious faith in technological progress, with our glorification of our own greed and violence always rationalized by our indignation at the greed and violence of others, until our land, our world, and ourselves are utterly destroyed. We know from history that massive human failure is possible. It is foolish to assume that we will save ourselves from any fate that we have made possible simply because we have the conceit to call ourselves *Homo sapiens*.

On the other hand, we want to be hopeful, and hope is one of our duties. A part of our obligation to our own being and to our descendants is to study our life and our condition, searching always for the authentic underpinnings of hope. And if we look, these underpinnings can still be found.

For one thing, though we have caused the earth to be seriously diseased, it is not yet without health. The earth we have before us now is still abounding and beautiful. We must learn again to see that present world for what it is. The health of nature is the primary ground of hope—if we can find the humility and wisdom to accept nature as our teacher. The pattern of land stewardship is set by nature. This is why we must have stable rural economies and communities; we must keep alive in every place the human knowledge of the nature of that place. Nature is the best farmer and forester, for she does not destroy the land in order to make it productive. And so in our wish to preserve our land, we are not without the necessary lessons, nor are we without instruction, in our cultural and religious tradition, necessary to learn those lessons.

But we have not only the example of nature; we have still, though few and widely scattered, sufficient examples of competent and loving human stewardship of the earth. We have, too, our own desire to be healthy in a healthy world. Surely, most of us still have, somewhere within us, the fundamental human wish to die in a world in which we have been glad to live. And we *are*, in spite of much evidence to the contrary, somewhat sapient. We *can* think—if we will. If we know carefully enough who, what, and where we are, and if we keep the scale of our work small enough, we can think responsibly.

These assets are not the gigantic, technical, and costly equipment that we tend to think we need, but they are enough. They are, in fact, God's plenty. Because we have these assets, which are the supports of our legitimate hope, we can start from where we are, with what we have, and imagine and work for the healings that are necessary.

But we must begin by giving up any idea that we can bring about these healings without fundamental changes in the way we think and live. We face a choice that is starkly simple: we must change or be changed. If we fail to change for the better, then we will be changed for the worse. We cannot blunder our way into health by the same sad and foolish hopes by which we have blundered into disease. We must see that the standardless aims of industrial communism and industrial capitalism equally have failed. The aims of productivity, profitability, efficiency, limitless growth, limitless wealth, limitless power, limitless mechanization and automation can enrich and empower the few (for a while), but they will sooner or later ruin us all. The gross national product and the corporate bottom line are utterly meaningless as measures of the prosperity or health of the country.

If we want to succeed in our dearest aims and hopes as a people, we must understand that we cannot proceed any further without standards, and we must see that ultimately the standards are not set by us but by nature. We must see that it is foolish, sinful, and suicidal to destroy the health of nature for the sake of an economy that is really not an economy at all but merely a financial system, one that is unnatural, undemocratic, sacrilegious, and ephemeral. We must see the error of our effort to live by fire, by burning the world in order to live in it. There is no plainer symptom of our insanity than our avowed intention to maintain by fire an unlimited economic growth. Fire destroys what nourishes it and so in fact imposes severe limits on any growth associated with it. The true source and analogue of our economic life is the economy of plants, which never exceeds natural limits, never grows beyond the power of its place to support it, produces no waste, and enriches and preserves itself by death and decay. We must learn to grow like a tree, not like a fire. We must repudiate what Edward Abbey called "the ideology of the cancer cell": the idiotic ideology of "unlimited economic growth" that pushes blindly toward the limitation of massive catastrophe.

We must give up also our superstitious conviction that we can contrive technological solutions to all our problems. Soil loss, for example, is a problem that embarrasses all of our technological pretensions. If soil were all being lost in a huge slab somewhere, that would appeal to the would-be heroes of "science and technology," who might conceivably engineer a glamorous, large, and speedy solution—however many new problems they might cause in doing so. But soil is not usually lost in slabs or heaps of magnificent tonnage. It is lost a little at a time over millions of acres by the careless acts of millions of people. It cannot be saved by heroic feats of gigantic technology but only by millions of small acts and restraints, conditioned by small fidelities, skills, and desires. Soil loss is ultimately a cultural problem; it will be corrected only by cultural solutions.

The aims of production, profit, efficiency, economic growth, and technological progress imply, as I have said, no social or ecological standards, and in practice they submit to none. But there is another set of aims that does imply a standard, and these aims are freedom (which is pretty much a synonym for personal and local self-sufficiency), pleasure (that is, our gladness to be alive), and longevity or sustainability (by which we signify our wish that human freedom and pleasure may last). The standard implied by all of these aims is health. They depend ultimately and inescapably on the health of nature; the idea that freedom and pleasure can last long in a diseased world is preposterous. But these good things depend also on the health of human culture, and human culture is to a considerable extent the knowledge of economic and other domestic procedures—that is, ways of work, pleasure, and education—that preserve the health of nature.

In talking about health, we have thus begun to talk about community. But we must take care to see how this standard of health enlarges and clarifies the idea of community. If we speak of a *healthy* community, we cannot be speaking of a community that is merely human. We are talking about a neighborhood of humans in a place, plus the place itself: its soil, its water, its air, and all the families and tribes of the nonhuman creatures that belong to it. If the place is well preserved, if its entire membership, natural and human, is present in it, and if the human economy is in practical harmony with the nature of the place, then the community is healthy. A diseased community will be suffering natural losses that become, in turn, human losses. A healthy community is sustainable; it is, within reasonable limits, self-sufficient and, within reasonable limits, self-determined—that is, free of tyranny.

Community, then, is an indispensable term in any discussion of the connection between people and land. A healthy community is a form that includes all the local things that are connected by the larger, ultimately mysterious form of the Creation. In speaking of community, then, we are speaking of a complex connection not only among human beings or between humans and their homeland but also between the human economy and nature, between forest or prairie and field or orchard, and between troublesome creatures and pleasant ones. *All* neighbors are included.

From the standpoint of such a community, any form of land abuse—a clear-cut, a strip mine, an overplowed or overgrazed field—is as alien and as threatening as it would be from the standpoint of an ecosystem. From such a standpoint, it would be plain that land abuse reduces the possibilities of local life, just as do chain stores, absentee owners, and consolidated schools.

One obvious advantage of such an idea of community is that it provides a common ground and a common goal between conservationists and small-scale land users. The long-standing division between conservationists and farmers, ranchers, and other private small-business people is distressing because it is to a considerable extent false. It is readily apparent that the economic forces that threaten the health of ecosystems and the survival of species are equally threatening to economic democracy and the survival of human neighborhoods.

I believe that the most necessary question now—

for conservationists, for small-scale farmers, ranchers, and businesspeople, for politicians interested in the survival of democracy, and for consumers—is this: What must be the economy of a healthy community based in agriculture or forestry? It *cannot* be the present colonial economy in which only "raw materials" are exported and *all* necessities and pleasures are imported. To be healthy, land-based communities will need to add value to local products, they will need to supply local demand, and they will need to be reasonably self-sufficient in food, energy, pleasure, and other basic requirements.

Once a person understands the necessity of healthy local communities and community economies, it becomes easy to imagine a range of reforms that might bring them into being.

It is at least conceivable that useful changes might be started or helped along by consumer demand in the cities. There is, for example, already evidence of a growing concern among urban consumers about the quality and the purity of food. Once this demand grows extensive and competent enough, it will have the power to change agriculture—if there is enough left of agriculture, by then, to be changed.

It is even conceivable that our people in Washington might make decisions tending toward sustainability and self-sufficiency in local economies. The federal government could do much to help, if it would. Its mere acknowledgment that problems exist would be a promising start.

But let us admit that urban consumers are not going to be well informed about their economic sources very soon and that a federal administration enlightened about the needs and problems of the countryside is not an immediate prospect.

The real improvements then must come, to a con- ✳
siderable extent, from the local communities themselves. We need local revision of our methods of land
use and production. We need to study and work together to reduce scale, reduce overhead, reduce industrial dependencies; we need to market and process local
products locally; we need to bring local economies into
harmony with local ecosystems so that we can live and
work with pleasure in the same places indefinitely; we
need to substitute ourselves, our neighborhoods, our
local resources, for expensive imported goods and services; we need to increase cooperation among all local
economic entities: households, farms, factories, banks,
consumers, and suppliers. If we are serious about reducing government and the burdens of government,
then we need to do so by returning economic self-
determination to the people. And we must not do this
by inviting destructive industries to provide "jobs" in
the community; we must do it by fostering economic
democracy. For example, as much as possible of the
food that is consumed locally ought to be locally produced on small farms, and then processed in small, non-
polluting plants that are locally owned. We must do
everything possible to provide to ordinary citizens the
opportunity to own a small, usable share of the country.
In that way, we will put local capital to work locally,
not to exploit and destroy the land but to use it well.
This is not work just for the privileged, the well-
positioned, the wealthy, and the powerful. It is work
for everybody.

I acknowledge that to advocate such reforms is to
advocate a kind of secession—not a secession of armed
violence but a quiet secession by which people find the
practical means and the strength of spirit to remove

themselves from an economy that is exploiting them and destroying their homeland. The great, greedy, indifferent national and international economy is killing rural America, just as it is killing America's cities—it is killing our country. Experience has shown that there is no use in appealing to this economy for mercy toward the earth or toward any human community. All true patriots must find ways of opposing it.

—1991

OUT OF YOUR CAR,
OFF YOUR HORSE

*Twenty-seven Propositions About Global Thinking
and the Sustainability of Cities*

1. Properly speaking, global thinking is not possible. Those who have "thought globally" (and among them the most successful have been imperial governments and multinational corporations) have done so by means of simplifications too extreme and oppressive to merit the name of thought. Global thinkers have been and will be dangerous people. National thinkers tend to be dangerous also: we now have national thinkers in the northeastern United States who look on Kentucky as a garbage dump. A landfill in my county receives daily many truckloads of garbage from New York, New Jersey, and Pennsylvania. This is evidently all right with everybody but those of us who live here.

II. Global thinking can only be statistical. Its shallowness is exposed by the least intention to do something. Unless one is willing to be destructive on a very large scale, one cannot do something except locally, in a small place. Global thinking can only do to the globe what a space satellite does to it: reduce it, make a bauble of it. Look at one of those photographs of half the earth taken from outer space, and see if you recognize your neighborhood. If you want to *see* where you are, you will have to get out of your spaceship, out of your car, off your horse, and walk over the ground. On foot you will find that the earth is still satisfyingly large and full of beguiling nooks and crannies.

III. If we could think locally, we would take far better care of things than we do now. The right local questions and answers will be the right global ones. The Amish question "What will this do to our community?" tends toward the right answer for the world.

IV. If we want to put local life in proper relation to the globe, we must do so by imagination, charity, and forbearance and by making local life as competent, independent, and self-sufficient as possible —not by the presumptuous abstractions of "global thought."

V. If we want to keep our thoughts and acts from destroying the globe, then we must see to it that we do not ask too much of the globe or of any part of it. To make sure that we do not ask too much, we must learn to live at home, as independently and self-sufficiently as we can. This is the only way we can keep the land we are using and its ecological limits always in sight.

vi. The only sustainable city—and this, to me, is the indispensable ideal and goal—is a city in balance with its countryside: a city, that is, that would live off the *net* ecological income of its supporting region, paying as it goes all its ecological and human debts.

vii. The cities we now have are living off ecological principal and by economic assumptions that seem certain to destroy them. The people of these cities do not "live at home." They do not have their own supporting regions. They are out of balance with their supports, wherever on the globe their supports are.

viii. The balance between city and countryside is destroyed by industrial machinery, "cheap" productivity in field and forest, and "cheap" transportation. Rome destroyed the balance with slave labor; we have destroyed it with machines and "cheap" fossil fuel.

ix. Since the Civil War, perhaps, and certainly since World War II, the norms of productivity have been set by the fossil-fuel industries.

x. Geographically, the sources of the fossil fuels are rural. Technically, however, the production of these fuels is industrial and urban. The facts and integrities of local life and the principle of community are considered as little as possible, for to consider them would not be quickly profitable. Fossil fuels have always been produced at the expense of local ecosystems and of local human communities. The fossil-fuel economy is the industrial economy par excellence, and it assigns no value to local life, natural or human.

xi. When the industrial principles exemplified in fossil-fuel production are applied to field and forest, the results are identical: local life, both natural and human, is destroyed.

xii. Industrial procedures have been imposed on the countryside pretty much to the extent that country people have been seduced or forced into dependence on the industrial economy. By encouraging this dependence, corporations have increased their ability to rob the people of their property and their labor. The result is that a very small number of people now own all the usable property in the country, and workers are increasingly the hostages of their employers.

xiii. Our present "leaders"—the people of wealth and power—do not know what it means to take a place seriously: to think it worthy, for its own sake, of love and study and careful work. They cannot take any place seriously because they must be ready at any moment, by the terms of power and wealth in the modern world, to destroy any place.

xiv. Ecological good sense will be opposed by all the most powerful economic entities of our time, because ecological good sense requires the reduction or replacement of those entities. If ecological good sense is to prevail, it can do so only through the work and the will of the people and of the local communities.

xv. For this task, our currently prevailing assumptions about knowledge, information, education, money, and political will are inadequate. All the institutions with which I am familiar have adopted the organizational patterns and the quantitative measures of the industrial corporations. *Both* sides of the ecological debate, perhaps as a consequence, are alarmingly abstract.

xvi. But abstraction, of course, is what is wrong. The evil of the industrial economy (capitalist or communist) is the abstractness inherent in its procedures—its inability to distinguish one place or person or creature from another. William Blake saw this two hundred years ago. Anyone can see it now in the application of almost any of our common industrial tools and weapons.

xvii. Abstraction is the enemy *wherever* it is found. The abstractions of sustainability can ruin the world just as surely as the abstractions of industrial economics. Local life may be as much endangered by those who would "save the planet" as by those who would "conquer the world." For "saving the planet" calls for abstract purposes and central powers that cannot know—and thus will destroy—the integrity of local nature and local community.

xviii. In order to make ecological good sense for the planet, you must make ecological good sense locally. You *can't* act locally by thinking globally.

xix. No one can make ecological good sense for the planet. Everyone can make ecological good sense locally, *if* the affection, the scale, the knowledge, the tools, and the skills are right.

xx. The right scale in work gives power to affection. When one works beyond the reach of one's love for the place one is working in and for the things and creatures one is working with and among, then destruction inevitably results. An adequate local culture, among other things, keeps work within the reach of love.

xxi. The question before us, then, is an extremely difficult one: How do we begin to remake, or to make, a local culture that will preserve our part of the world while we use it? We are talking here not just about a kind of knowledge that *involves* affection but also about a kind of knowledge that comes from or with affection—knowledge that is unavailable to the unaffectionate and that is unavailable to anyone in the form of "information."

xxii. What, for a start, might be the economic result of local affection? We don't know. Moreover, we are probably never going to know in any way that would satisfy the average dean or corporate executive. The ways of love tend to be secretive and, even to the lovers themselves, somewhat inscrutable.

xxiii. The real work of planet-saving will be small, humble, and humbling, and (insofar as it involves love) pleasing and rewarding. Its jobs will be too many to count, too many to report, too many to be publicly noticed or rewarded, too small to make anyone rich or famous.

xxiv. The great obstacle may be not greed but the modern hankering after glamour. A lot of our smartest, most concerned people want to come up with a big solution to a big problem. I don't think that planet-saving, if we take it seriously, can furnish employment to many such people.

xxv. When I think of the kind of worker the job requires, I think of Dorothy Day (if one can think of Dorothy Day herself, separate from the publicity that came as a result of her rarity), a person willing to go down and down into the daunting, humbling, almost hopeless local presence of the problem—to face the great problem one small life at a time.

xxvi. Some cities can never be sustainable at their present levels of population because they do not have a countryside around them or near them from which they can be sustained. New York City cannot be made sustainable, nor can Phoenix. Some cities in Kentucky or the Midwest, on the other hand, might reasonably hope to become sustainable.

xxvii. To make a sustainable city, one must begin somehow and I think the beginning must be small and economic. A beginning could be made, for example, by increasing the amount of food bought from farmers in the local countryside by consumers in the city. As the food economy became more local, local farming would become more diverse; the farms would become smaller, more complex in structure, more productive; and some city people would be needed to work on the farms. Sooner or later, as a means of reducing expenses both ways, organic wastes from the city would go out to fertilize the farms of the supporting region; thus, city people would have to assume an agricultural responsibility and would be properly motivated to do so both by the wish to have a dependable supply of excellent food and by the fear of contaminating that supply. The increase of economic intimacy between a city and its sources would change minds (assuming, of course, that the minds in question would stay put long enough to be changed). It would improve minds. The locality, by becoming partly sustainable, would produce the thought it would need to become more sustainable.

—1991

CONSERVATION IS
GOOD WORK

There are, as nearly as I can make out, three kinds of conservation currently operating. The first is the preservation of places that are grandly wild or "scenic" or in some other way spectacular. The second is what is called "conservation of natural resources"—that is, of the things of nature that we intend to use: soil, water, timber, and minerals. The third is what you might call industrial troubleshooting: the attempt to limit or stop or remedy the most flagrant abuses of the industrial system. All three kinds of conservation are inadequate, both separately and together.

Right at the heart of American conservation, from the beginning, has been the preservation of spectacular places. The typical American park is in a place that is "breathtakingly" beautiful or wonderful and of little apparent economic value. Mountains, canyons, deserts, spectacular landforms, geysers, waterfalls—these are the stuff of parks. There is, significantly, no prairie national park. Wilderness preserves, as Dave Foreman points out, tend to include much "rock and ice" and

little marketable timber. Farmable land, in general, has
tempted nobody to make a park. Wes Jackson has com-
mented with some anxiety on the people who charge
blindly across Kansas and eastern Colorado, headed for
the mountains west of Denver. These are nature lovers
and sightseers, but they are utterly oblivious of or bored
by the rich natural and human history of the Plains.
The point of Wes Jackson's anxiety is that the love of
nature that limits itself to the love of places that are
"scenic" is implicitly dangerous. It is dangerous because
it tends to exclude unscenic places from nature and from
the respect that we sometimes accord to nature. This
is why so much of the landscape that is productively
used is also abused; it is used solely according to standards dictated by the financial system and not at all
according to standards dictated by the nature of the
place. Moreover, as we are beginning to see, it is going
to be extremely difficult to make enough parks to preserve vulnerable species and the health of ecosystems
or large watersheds.

"Natural resources," the part of nature that we are
going to use, is the part outside the parks and preserves
(which, of course, we also use). But "conservation of
natural resources" is now in confusion because it is a
concept that has received much lip service but not much
thought or practice. Part of the confusion is caused by
thinking of "natural resources" as belonging to one category when, in fact, they belong to two: surface resources, like soils and forests, which can be preserved
in use; and underground resources, like coal or oil,
which cannot be. The one way to conserve the minable
fuels and materials that use inevitably exhausts is to
limit use. At present, we have no intention of limiting
such use, and so we cannot say that we are at all in-

terested in the conservation of exhaustible resources. Surface or renewable resources, on the other hand, can be preserved in use so that their yield is indefinitely sustainable.

Sustainability is a hopeful concept not only because it is a present necessity but because it has a history. We know, for example, that some agricultural soils have been preserved in continuous use for several thousand years. We know, moreover, that it is possible to improve soil in use. And it is clear that a forest can be used in such a way that it remains a forest, with its biological communities intact and its soil undamaged, while producing a yield of timber. But the methods by which exhaustible resources are extracted and used have set the pattern also for the use of sustainable resources, with the result that now soils and forests are not merely being used but are being used up, exactly as coal seams are used up.

Since the sustainable use of renewable resources depends on the existence of settled, small local economies and communities capable of preserving the local knowledge necessary for good farming and forestry, it is obvious that there is no simple, easy, or quick answer to the problem of the exhaustion of sustainable resources. We probably are not going to be able to conserve natural resources so long as our extraction and use of the goods of nature are wasteful and improperly scaled, or so long as these resources are owned or controlled by absentees, or so long as the standard of extraction and use is profitability rather than the health of natural and human communities.

Because we are living in an era of ecological crisis, it is understandable that much of our attention, anxiety, and energy is focused on exceptional cases, the outrages and extreme abuses of the industrial economy: global warming, the global assault on the last remnants of wilderness, the extinction of species, oil spills, chemical spills, Love Canal, Bhopal, Chernobyl, the burning oil fields of Kuwait. But a conservation effort that concentrates only on the extremes of industrial abuse tends to suggest that the only abuses are the extreme ones when, in fact, the earth is probably suffering more from many small abuses than from a few large ones. By treating the spectacular abuses as exceptional, the powers that be would like to keep us from seeing that the industrial system (capitalist or communist or socialist) is in itself and by necessity of all of its assumptions extremely dangerous and damaging and that it exists to support an extremely dangerous and damaging way of life. The large abuses exist within and because of a pattern of smaller abuses.

Much of the Sacramento River is now dead because a carload of agricultural poison was spilled into it. The powers that be would like us to believe that this colossal "accident" was an exception in a general pattern of safe use. Diluted and used according to the instructions on the label, they will tell us, the product that was spilled is harmless. They neglect to acknowledge any of the implications that surround the accident: that if this product is to be used in dilution almost everywhere, it will have to be manufactured, stored, and transported in concentration somewhere; that even in "harmless" dilution, such chemicals are getting into the water, the air, the rain, and into the bodies of animals and people; that when such a product is distributed to the general public, it will inevitably be spilled in its concentrated form in large or small quantities and that such "accidents" are anticipated, discounted as "acceptable risk," and charged to nature and society by the powers that be; that such chemicals are needed, in the first place, because the scale, the methods, and the economy of American agriculture are all monstrously out of kilter; that such chemicals are used to replace the work and intelligence of people; and that such a deformed agriculture is made necessary, in the first place, by the public's demand for a diet that is at once cheap and luxurious—too cheap to support adequate agricultural communities or good agricultural methods or good maintenance of agricultural land and yet so goofily self-indulgent as to demand, in every season, out-of-season foods produced by earth-destroying machines and chemicals.

We tend to forget, too, in our just and necessary outrage at the government-led attack on public lands and the last large tracts of wilderness, that for the very same reasons and to the profit of the very same people, thousands of woodlots are being abusively and wastefully logged.

Here, then, are three kinds of conservation, all of them urgently necessary and all of them failing. Conservationists have won enough victories to give them heart and hope and a kind of accreditation, but they know better than anybody how immense and how baffling their task has become. For all their efforts, our soils and waters, forests and grasslands are being used up. Kinds of creatures, kinds of human life, good natural and human possibilities are being destroyed. Nothing now exists anywhere on earth that is not under threat of human destruction. Poisons are everywhere. Junk is everywhere.

These dangers are large and public, and they inev-

itably cause us to think of changing public policy. This
is good, so far as it goes. There should be no relenting
in our efforts to influence politics and politicians. But
in the name of honesty and sanity we must recognize
the limits of politics. It is, after all, much easier to
improve a policy than it is to improve the community
the policy attempts to affect. And it is also probable
that some changes required by conservation cannot be
politically made and that some necessary changes will
have to be made by the governed without the help or
approval of the government.

I must admit here that my experience over more
than twenty years as part of an effort to influence agricultural policy has not been encouraging. Our arguments directed at the government and the universities
by now remind me of the ant crawling up the buttocks
of the elephant with love on his mind. We have not
made much impression. My conclusion, I imagine, is
the same as the ant's, for these great projects, once
undertaken, are hard to abandon: we have got to get
more radical.

However destructive may be the policies of the government and the methods and products of the corporations, the root of the problem is always to be found
in private life. We must learn to see that every problem
that concerns us as conservationists always leads straight
to the question of how we live. The world is being
destroyed, no doubt about it, by the greed of the rich
and powerful. It is also being destroyed by popular
demand. There are not enough rich and powerful people
to consume the whole world; for that, the rich and
powerful need the help of countless ordinary people.
We acquiesce in the wastefulness and destructiveness
of the national and global economics by acquiescing in

the wastefulness and destructiveness of our own households and communities. If conservation is to have a hope of succeeding, then conservationists, while continuing their effort to change public life, are going to have to begin the effort to change private life as well.

The problems we are worried about are caused not just by other people but by ourselves. And this realization should lead directly to two more. The first is that solving these problems is not work merely for so-called environmental organizations and agencies but also for individuals, families, and local communities. We are used to hearing about turning off unused lights, putting a brick in the toilet tank, using water-saving shower heads, setting the thermostat low, sharing rides, and so forth—pretty dull stuff. But I'm talking about actual jobs of work that are interesting because they require intelligence and because they are accomplished in response to interesting questions: What are the principles of household economy, and how can they be applied under present circumstances? What are the principles of a neighborhood or a local economy, and how can they be applied under present circumstances? What do people already possess in their minds and bodies, in their families and neighborhoods, in their dwellings and in their local landscape, that can replace what is now being supplied by our consumptive and predatory so-called economy? What can we supply to ourselves cheaply or for nothing that we are now paying dearly for? To answer such questions requires more intelligence and involves more pleasure than all the technological breakthroughs of the last two hundred years.

Second, the realization that we ourselves, in our daily economic life, are causing the problems we are trying to solve ought to show us the inadequacy of the language we are using to talk about our connection to the world. The idea that we live in something called "the environment," for instance, is utterly preposterous. This word came into use because of the pretentiousness of learned experts who were embarrassed by the religious associations of "Creation" and who thought "world" too mundane. But "environment" means that which surrounds or encircles us; it means a world separate from ourselves, outside us. The real state of things, of course, is far more complex and intimate and interesting than that. The world that environs us, that is around us, is also within us. We are made of it; we eat, drink, and breathe it; it is bone of our bone and flesh of our flesh. It is also a Creation, a holy mystery, made for and to some extent by creatures, some but by no means all of whom are humans. This world, this Creation, belongs in a limited sense to us, for we may rightfully require certain things of it—the things necessary to keep us fully alive as the kind of creature we are—but we also belong to it, and it makes certain rightful claims on us: that we care properly for it, that we leave it undiminished not just to our children but to all the creatures who will live in it after us. None of this intimacy and responsibility is conveyed by the word *environment*.

That word is a typical product of the old dualism that is at the root of most of our ecological destructiveness. So, of course, is "biocentrism." If life is at the center, what is at the periphery? And for that matter, *where* is the periphery? "Deep ecology," another bifurcating term, implies that there is, a couple of layers up, a shallow ecology that is not so good—or that an ecosystem is a sort of layer cake with the icing on the bottom. Not only is this language incapable of giving a true description of our relation to the world; it is also academic, artificial, and pretentious. It is the sort of language used by a visiting expert who does not want the local people to ask any questions. (I am myself an anthropobiotheointerpenetrist and a gastrointeroenvironmentalist, but I am careful to say so only in the company of other experts.)

No settled family or community has ever called its home place an "environment." None has ever called its feeling for its home place "biocentric" or "anthropocentric." None has ever thought of its connection to its home place as "ecological," deep or shallow. The concepts and insights of the ecologists are of great usefulness in our predicament, and we can hardly escape the need to speak of "ecology" and "ecosystems." But the terms themselves are culturally sterile. They come from the juiceless, abstract intellectuality of the universities which was invented to disconnect, displace, and disembody the mind. The real names of the environment are the names of rivers and river valleys; creeks, ridges, and mountains; towns and cities; lakes, woodlands, lanes, roads, creatures, and people.

And the real name of our connection to this everywhere different and differently named earth is "work." We are connected by work even to the places where we don't work, for all places are connected; it is clear by now that we cannot exempt one place from our ruin of another. The name of our *proper* connection to the earth is "good work," for good work involves much giving of honor. It honors the source of its materials; it honors the place where it is done; it honors the art by which it is done; it honors the thing that it makes and the user of the made thing. Good work is always modestly scaled, for it cannot ignore either the nature of individual places or the differences between places, and it always involves a sort of religious humility, for not everything is known. Good work can be defined only in particularity, for it must be defined a little differently for every one of the places and every one of the workers on the earth.

The name of our present society's connection to the earth is "bad work"—work that is only generally and crudely defined, that enacts a dependence that is ill understood, that enacts no affection and gives no honor. Every one of us is to some extent guilty of this bad work. This guilt does not mean that we must indulge in a lot of breast-beating and confession; it means only that there is much good work to be done by every one of us and that we must begin to do it. All of us are responsible for bad work, not so much because we do it ourselves (though we all do it) as because we have it done for us by other people.

Here we are bound to see our difficulty as almost overwhelming. What proxies have we issued, and to whom, to use the earth on our behalf? How, in this global economy, are we to render anything like an accurate geographical account of our personal economies? How do we take our lives from this earth that we are so anxious to protect and restore to health?

Most of us get almost all the things we need by buying them; most of us know only vaguely, if at all, where those things come from; and most of us know not at all what damage is involved in their production. We are almost entirely dependent on an economy of which we are almost entirely ignorant. The provenance, for example, not only of the food we buy at the store but of the chemicals, fuels, metals, and other materials necessary to grow, harvest, transport, process, and package that food is almost necessarily a mystery to us. To know the full economic history of a head of supermarket cauliflower would require an immense job of research. To be so completely and so ignorantly dependent on the present abusive food economy certainly defines us as earth abusers. It also defines us as potential victims.

Living as we now do in almost complete dependence on a global economy, we are put inevitably into a position of ignorance and irresponsibility. No one can know the whole globe. We can connect ourselves to the globe as a whole only by means of a global economy that, without knowing the earth, plunders it for us. The global economy (like the national economy before it) operates on the superstition that the deficiencies or needs or wishes of one place may safely be met by the ruination of another place. To build houses here, we clear-cut the forests there. To have air-conditioning here, we strip-mine the mountains there. To drive our cars here, we sink our oil wells there. It is an absentee economy. Most people aren't using or destroying what they can see. If we cannot see our garbage or the grave we have dug with our energy proxies, then we assume that all is well. The issues of carrying capacity and population remain abstract and not very threatening to most people for the same reason. If this nation or region cannot feed its population, then food can be imported from other nations or regions. All the critical questions affecting our use of the earth are left to be answered by "the market" or the law of supply and demand, which proposes no limit on either supply or demand. An economy without limits is an economy without discipline.

Conservationists of all kinds would agree, I think,

that no discipline, public or private, is implied by the industrial economy and that none is practiced by it. The implicit wish of the industrial economy is that producers might be wasteful, shoddy, and irresponsible and that consumers might be gullible, extravagant, and irresponsible. To fulfill this wish, the industrial economy employs an immense corps of hireling politicians, publicists, lobbyists, admen, and adwomen. The consequent ruin is notorious: we have been talking about it for generations; it brought conservation into being. And conservationists have learned very well how to address this ruin as a public problem. There is now no end to the meetings and publications in which the horrifying statistics are recited, usually with the conclusion that pressure should be put on the government to do something. Often, this pressure has been applied, and the government has done something. But the government has not done enough and may never do enough. It is likely that the government *cannot* do enough.

The government's disinclination to do more than it does is explained, of course, by the government's bought-and-paid-for servitude to interests that do not want it to do more. But there may also be a limit of another kind: a government that could do enough, assuming it had the will, would almost certainly be a government radically and unpleasantly different from the one prescribed by our Constitution. A government undertaking to protect all of nature that is now abused or threatened would have to take total control of the country. Police and bureaucrats—and opportunities for malfeasance—would be everywhere. To wish only for a public or a political solution to the problem of conservation may be to wish for a solution as bad as the problem and still be unable to solve it.

The way out of this dilemma is to understand the ruin of nature as a problem that is both public and private. The failure of public discipline in matters of economy is only the other face of the failure of private discipline. If we have worked at the issues of public policy so long and so exclusively as to bring political limits into sight, then let us turn—not instead but also—to issues of private economy and see how far we can go in that direction. It is a direction that may take us further and produce more satisfactory and lasting results than the direction of policy.

The dilemma of private economic responsibility, as I have said, is that we have allowed our suppliers to enlarge our economic boundaries so far that we cannot be responsible for our effects on the world. The only remedy for this that I can see is to draw in our economic boundaries, shorten our supply lines, so as to permit us literally to know where we are economically. The closer we live to the ground that we live from, the more we will know about our economic life; the more we know about our economic life, the more able we will be to take responsibility for it. The way to bring discipline into one's personal or household or community economy is to limit one's economic geography.

This obviously opens up an agenda almost as daunting as the political agenda. The difference—a consoling one—is that when we try to influence policy, only large jobs must be done; whereas when we seek to reform private economies, the work is necessarily modest, and it can be started by anybody anywhere. What is required is the formation of local economic strategies—and eventually of local economies—by which to resist abuses of natural and human communities by the larger economy. And, of course, in talking about the formation of local economies capable of using an earthly place without ruining it, we are talking about the reformation of people; we are talking about reviving good work as an economic force.

If we think of this task of rebuilding local economies as one large task that must be done in a hurry, then we will again be overwhelmed and will want the government to do it. If, on the other hand, we define the task as beginning the reformation of our private or household economies, then the way is plain. What we must do is use well the considerable power we have as consumers: the power of choice. We can choose to buy or not to buy, and we can choose what to buy. The standard by which we choose must be the health of the community—and by that we must mean the *whole* community: ourselves, the place where we live, and all the humans and other creatures who live there with us. In a healthy community, people will be richer in their neighbors, in neighborhood, in the health and pleasure of neighborhood, than in their bank accounts. It is better, therefore, even if the cost is greater, to buy near at hand than to buy at a distance. It is better to buy from a small, privately owned local store than from a chain store. It is better to buy a good product than a bad one. Do not buy anything you don't need. Do as much as you can for yourself. If you cannot do something for yourself, see if you have a neighbor who can do it for you. Do everything you can to see that your money stays as long as possible in the local community. If you have money to invest, try to invest it locally, both to help the local community and to keep from helping the larger economy that is destroying local communities. Begin to ask yourself how your money could be put at minimal interest into the hands of a young person who wants to start a farm, a store, a shop, or a small business that the community needs. This agenda can be followed by individuals and single families. If it is followed by people in groups—churches, conservation organizations, neighborhood associations, groups of small farmers, and the like—the possibilities multiply and the effects will be larger.

The economic system that most affects the health of the world and that may be most subject to consumer influence is that of food. And the issue of food provides an excellent example of what I am talking about. If you want to reform your own food economy, you can make a start without anybody's permission or help. If you have a place to do it, grow some food for yourself. Growing some of your own food gives you pleasure, exercise, knowledge, sales resistance, and standards. Your own food, if you grow it the right way, will taste good and so will cause you to wish to buy food that tastes good. So far as you can, buy food that is locally grown. Tell your grocer that you are interested in locally grown food. If you can't find locally grown food in stores, then see if you can deal directly with a local farmer. The value of this, for conservationists, is that when consumers are acquainted and friendly with their producers, they can influence production. They can know the land on which their food is produced. They can refuse to buy food that is produced with dangerous chemicals or by other destructive practices. As these connections develop, local agriculture will diversify, become more healthy and more stable, employ more people. As local demand increases and becomes more knowledgeable, small food-processing industries will enter the local economy. Everything that is done by the standard of community health will make new possibilities for good work—that is for the responsible use of the world.

The forest economy is not so obviously subject to consumer influence, but such influence is sorely needed. Both the forests themselves and their human communities suffer for the want of local forest economies—properly scaled wood-products industries that would be the basis of stable communities and would provide local incentives for the good use of the forest. People who see that they must depend on the forest for generations, in a complex local forest economy, will want the forest to last and be healthy; they will *not* want to see all the marketable timber ripped out of it as fast as possible. Both forest and farm communities would benefit from technologies that could be locally supplied and maintained. Draft horses, for example, are better than large machines, both for the woods and for the local economy.

The economy of recreation has hardly been touched as an issue of local economy and conservation, though conservationists and consumers alike have much to gain from making it such an issue. At present, there is an almost complete disconnection between the economic use of privately owned farm and forest land and its use for recreation. Such land is now much used by urban people for hunting and fishing, but mainly without benefit to the landowners, who therefore receive no incentive from this use to preserve wildlife habitat or to take the best care of their woodlands and stream margins. They need to receive such incentives. It is not beyond reason that public funds might be given to private landowners to preserve and enhance the recreational value —that is, the wildness—of their land. But since governments are unlikely to do this soon, the incentives need to be provided by consumer and conservation groups working in cooperation with farm groups. The rule of the food economy ought to apply to the recreation economy: find your pleasure and your rest as near home as possible. In Kentucky, for example, we have hundreds of miles of woodland stretching continuously along the sides of our creek and river valleys. Why should conservation and outdoor groups not pay an appropriate price to farmers to maintain hiking trails and campsites and preserve the forests in such places? The money that would carry a family to a vacation in a distant national park could thus be kept at home and used to help the local economy and protect the local countryside.

The point of all this is the use of local buying power, local gumption, and local affection to see that the best care is taken of the local land. This sort of effort would bridge the gap, now so destructive, between the conservationists and the small farmers and ranchers, and that would be one of its great political benefits. But the fundamental benefit would be to the world and ourselves. We would begin to protect the world not just by conserving it but also by living in it.

—1991

A BAD BIG IDEA

After World War II, the United States and seventeen other nations entered into the General Agreement on Tariffs and Trade (also known as GATT) for the purpose of regulating international trade and resolving international trade disputes. Beginning in 1986, with the so-called Uruguay round of GATT negotiations, the Reagan and Bush administrations, working mostly in secret, undertook to make a set of changes in GATT that would have dire economic and ecological effects on the more than one hundred nations now subscribing to the agreement—and that would significantly reduce the freedom of their citizens as well. Whether or not the Clinton administration will continue the Reagan-Bush agitation for these changes remains to be seen.

The U.S. proposals on agriculture were drafted mostly by Daniel Amstutz, formerly a Cargill executive, and they are backed by other large supranational corporations. Made to order for the grain traders and agrochemical companies that operate in the "global economy," these proposals aim both to eliminate farm price supports and production controls and to attempt to force all member nations to conform to health and safety standards that would be set in Rome by Codex Alimentarius, a group of international scientific bureaucrats that is under the influence of the agribusiness corporations. Pressure for these revisions has come solely from these corporations and their allies. There certainly has been no popular movement in favor of them—not in any country—although there have been some popular movements in opposition.

When very important persons have plunder in mind, they characteristically invent ugly euphemisms for what they intend to do, and the promoters of these GATT revisions are no exception:

Tariffication refers to the recommended process by which all controls on imports of agricultural products will be replaced by tariffs, which will then be reduced or eliminated within five to ten years. This would have the effect of opening U.S. markets (and all others) to unlimited imports.

Harmonization refers to a process by which the standards of trade among the member nations would be brought into "harmony." This would mean lowering all those standards regulating food safety, toxic residues, inspections, packaging and labeling, and so on that are higher than the standards set by Codex Alimentarius.

And *fast track* refers to a capitulation by which our Congress has ceded to the president the authority to make an international trade agreement and to draft the enabling legislation, which then is not subject to congressional amendment and which must be accepted or rejected as a whole within ninety session days.

If the proposed revisions in the GATT are adopted,

every farmer in every member nation will be thrown into competition with every other farmer. With restrictions lowered to international minimums and with farmers under increasing pressure to make up in volume for drastically reduced unit prices, this will become a competition in land exploitation. Such conservation practices as are now in use (and they are already inadequate) will of necessity be abandoned; land rape and the use of toxic chemicals will increase, as will the exploitation of people. American farmers, who must continue to buy their expensive labor-replacing machines, fuel, and chemicals on markets entirely controlled by the suppliers, will be forced to market their products in competition with the cheapest hand labor of the poor countries. And the poor countries, needing to feed their own people, will see the food vacuumed off their plates by lucrative export markets. The supranational corporations, meanwhile, will be able to slide about at will over the face of the globe to wherever products can be bought cheapest and sold highest.

It is easy to see who will have the freedom in this international "free market." The proposed GATT revisions, as one of their advocates has said, are "exactly what exporters need"—the assumption being, as usual, that what is good for exporters is good for everybody. But what is good for exporters is by no means necessarily good for producers, and in fact these proposed revisions expose a long-standing difference of interest between farmers and agribusiness marketers. We in the United States have seen how unrestrained competition among farmers, increasing surpluses and driving down prices, has directly served the purposes of the agribusiness corporations. These corporations have, in fact, remained hugely and consistently profitable right through an era of severe economic hardship in rural America. They are clearly in a position to take excellent advantage of "free-market" competition, for the proposed GATT revisions would permit them to practice the same exploitation without restraint in the world at large.

What these proposals actually propose is a revolution as audacious, far-reaching, and sudden as any the world has seen. Though they would deny to the people of some 108 nations any choice in the matter of protecting their land, their farmers, their food supply, or their health, these proposals were not drafted and, if adopted, would not be implemented by anybody elected by the people of any of the 108 nations. Their purpose is to bypass all local, state, and national governments in order to subordinate the interests of those governments and of the people they represent to the interests of a global "free market" run by a few supranational corporations. By this single device, if it should be implemented, these corporations would destroy the protections that have been won by generations of conservationists, labor organizers, consumer advocates—and by democrats and lovers of freedom. This is an unabashed attempt to replace government with economics and to destroy any sort of local (let alone personal) self-determination. The intended effect would be to centralize control of all prices and standards in the international food economy and to place this control in the hands of the corporations that are best able to profit from it. The revised GATT would thus be a license issued to a privileged few for an all-out economic assault on the lands and peoples of the world. It would establish a "free" global economy that would be a tighter enclosure than most Americans, at least, have so far experienced.

The issue here really is not whether international trade shall be free but whether or not it makes sense for a country—or, for that matter, a region—to destroy its own capacity to produce its own food. How can a government, entrusted with the safety and health of its people, conscientiously barter away in the name of an economic idea that people's ability to feed itself? And if people lose their ability to feed themselves, how can they be said to be free?

The supporters of these GATT revisions assume that there is no longer any possibility of escape from the global economy and, furthermore, that there is no need for such an escape. They assume that all nations are therefore already properly subservient to the global economy and that the highest purpose of national governments is to serve as attorneys for the supranational corporations. They assume also (like far too many farmers and consumers) that there is no possibility of a food economy that is not decided on "at the top" in some center of power.

But in so assuming, these people unwittingly have provided the rest of us with our best occasion so far to understand and to talk about the need for sound and reasonably self-sufficient local food economies. They have forced us to realize that politics and economics are in fact as inseparable as are economics and ecology. They have made it clear that if we want to be free, we will have to free ourselves somehow from the purposes of these great supranational concentrations of greed, wealth, and power. They have forced us to realize that a General Agreement on Tariffs and Trade may be able to set the standards for governments but that it cannot set the standards for individuals and local communities—unless those individuals and communities allow it

to do so. They have, in other words, made certain truths
self-evident.

The proposed GATT revisions offend against democracy and freedom, against people's natural concern
for bodily and ecological health, and against the very
possibility of a sustainable food supply. Apart from the
corporate ambition to gather the wealth and power of
the world into fewer and fewer hands, these revisions
make no sense, for they ignore or reduce to fantasy all
the realities with which they are concerned: ecological,
agricultural, economic, political, and cultural. Their
great evil originates in their underlying assumption that
all the world may safely be subjected to the desires and
controls of a centralizing power. For this is what "harmonization" really envisions: not the necessary small
local harmonies that actually can be made among neighbors and between people and their land but rather the
"harmony" that might exist between exploiter and exploited after all protest is silenced and all restraints abandoned. The would-be exploiters of the world would like
to assume—it would be so easy for them if they could
assume—that the world is everywhere uniform and con-
formable to their desires.

The world, on the contrary, is made up of an immense diversity of countries, climates, topographies,
regions, ecosystems, soils, and human cultures—so
many as to be endlessly frustrating to centralizing ambition, and this perhaps explains the attempt to impose
a legal uniformity on it. However, anybody who is
interested in real harmony, in economic and ecological
justice, will see immediately that such justice requires
not international uniformity but international generosity toward local diversity.

And anybody interested in solving, rather than

profiting from, the problems of food production and distribution will see that in the long run the safest food supply is a local food supply, not a supply that is dependent on a global economy. Nations and regions within nations must be left free—and should be encouraged—to develop the local food economies that best suit local needs and local conditions.

—1993

THE PROBLEM
OF TOBACCO

Though I would just as soon get along without it, an humbling awareness of the complexity of moral issues is said to be a good thing. If such an awareness is, in fact, good—and if I, in fact, have it—I have tobacco to thank for it. To many people nowadays, there is nothing complex about the moral issue of tobacco. They are simply against it. They will sit in their large automobiles, spewing a miasma of toxic gas into the atmosphere, and they will thank you for not smoking a cigarette. They will sit in a smoke-free bar, drinking stingers and other lethal beverages, and wonder how smokers can have so little respect for their bodies. They will complacently stand in the presence of a coal-fired power plant or a nuclear power plant or a bomb factory or a leaking chemical plant, and they will wonder how a tobacco farmer can have so little regard for public health. Well, as always, it matters whose ox is being gored. And tobacco, I am obliged to confess, is my ox.

I was born in tobacco country, into a family preoccupied with the cultivation, the economy, and the pol-

itics of tobacco. Many of my closest and dearest friends
have been and are tobacco growers. I have worked on
the crop from early childhood until now. I have liked
and often enjoyed the work. I love the crop in all its
stages. I think tobacco is a beautiful plant. I love the
lore and the conversation of tobacco growing. I love the
smell of tobacco and of tobacco smoke.

Burley tobacco, as I first knew it, was produced
with an intensity of care and a refinement of skill that
far exceeded that given to any food crop that I know
about. It was a handmade crop; between plant bed and
warehouse, every plant, every leaf, was looked at,
touched, appraised, lifted, and carried many times. The
experience of growing up in a community in which
virtually everybody was passionately interested in the
quality of a local product was, I now see, a rare privilege. As a boy and a young man, I worked with men
who were as fiercely insistent on the ways and standards
of their discipline as artists—which is what they were.
In those days, to be recognized as a "tobacco man" was
to be accorded an honor such as other cultures bestowed
on the finest hunters or warriors or poets. The accolade
"He's a *tobacco* man!" would be accompanied by a shake
of the head to indicate that such surpassing excellence
was, finally, a mystery; there was more to it than met
the eye.

It is hardly too much to say that we were a tobacco
culture. Our nationality was more or less American.
Our religion was nominally and sometimes approxi-
mately Christian. But our culture was largely determined by tobacco, just as the culture of the Plains
Indians was determined by the horse. It was our staple
crop, the cornerstone of our economy. Because of "the
program"—the federal regulations that limited produc-

tion in order to control price—the tobacco market was the only market on which the farmer was dependably not a victim. Though we practiced a diversified way of farming, our farming focused on tobacco. The rhythm of our farming year, as of our financial year, was set by the annual drama of the tobacco crop.

Because so much handwork was involved in the growing of tobacco, it was a very sociable crop. "Many hands make light work," people said, and so one of the most attractive customs of our tobacco culture was "swapping work." The times of hardest work were "setting," in the spring, when the plants were moved from the beds to the patches; "cutting," in late summer, when the plants were harvested and hung in curing barns; and "stripping," in the fall and winter, when the cured leaves were removed from the stalks, graded, and tied in "hands" for the market. At these times, neighbors helped each other in order to bring together the many hands that lightened work. Thus, these times of hardest work were also times of big meals and of much talk, storytelling, and laughter.

To me, this was a good kind of life, and it provided excellent experience for a boy. To work in the company of men and women who were superb workers, to learn their characters, to glean from their talk an intimate history of the people, farms, and fields that were one's true nationality—this was an education of inestimable value. To me, the tobacco patches and tobacco barns and stripping rooms of my native countryside have been an indispensable school. And so I cannot help but look on our tobacco culture with considerable affection and gratitude.

There is another, more practical benefit of tobacco that must be mentioned. For a sloping, easily eroded

countryside such as I live in and such as comprises much
of the "tobacco belt," tobacco has been an ideal crop,
because it has permitted significant income to be realized
from small acreages, thereby sparing us the inevitable
damage of extensive plowing, and because it has con-
formed well to the pattern of livestock farming. Tobacco, of course, has not been invariably kind to the
land; grown on steep hillsides, as it often was, it was
as damaging as any other row crop. But in general, I
believe that a considerable saving of soil can be attrib-
uted to tobacco. If tobacco farmers had attempted to
realize an equivalent income from corn, neither they
nor their fields would have lasted long.

Perhaps nobody brought up as I was can speak of
tobacco without at least some affection. I have said as
much good of it as I know. But of course everything to
be said about tobacco is not good. There have always
been people who disliked it. There has long been a vague
religious antipathy to it, though in tobacco country, to
date, churches have generally been glad enough to receive their tithes from it. Some have thought, and not
without justification, that smoking or chewing or dip-
ping is a "filthy habit." Though it was often said, when
I was a boy, that smoking would "stunt your growth,"
we did not know any smokers who had been stunted
—unless, perhaps, they had been intended to be giants.

Tobacco became an authentic moral issue only
within the last thirty years and for two reasons: the case
against it, as a serious threat to health, became extremely
persuasive; and in spite of this widely recognized threat,
tobacco has continued to be grown, and tobacco products continue to be advertised and sold. There is, in
my opinion, no way to deny that this is a most serious

moral predicament and no way to evade the questions raised by it or to lighten their gravity.

Because I have written a good bit about farmers who raise tobacco and because I have often spoken in defense of the tobacco program, I often fall into conversations on the subject with people who are indignant. These conversations are always fragmentary because of the great complexity of the subject, and I have never been satisfied with any of them. And so I would like now to attempt something like a complete dialogue:

"Do you smoke?" I am asked.

And I reply, "No."

"Did you ever smoke?"

"Yes, from about the age of fourteen until I was thirty."

"Why did you quit?"

"Two reasons. One, I had young children."

"So you do agree that smoking tobacco is unhealthy!"

"Yes, though I still have some questions on the subject. Since, for example, there is nobody today whose lungs are polluted *only* with tobacco smoke, I would like to know what contribution other pollutants may make to 'tobacco-caused' diseases. And since nobody now smokes chemical-free tobacco, I would like to know the effect of the residues of agricultural chemicals in the tobacco. But, yes, I do believe that smoke inhalation is unhealthy."

"But most modern smoke is inhaled unwillingly. Why would anyone willingly inhale smoke that is dangerous to health?"

"Well, to start with, sociability."

"Sociability?"

"Tobacco smoke is fragrant, and smoking at its best is convivial or ceremonious and pleasant. Some would say it is a comfort. But you haven't asked me my second reason for quitting."

"What was your second reason?"

"Addiction. I didn't like being addicted. I had got so I could smoke a cigarette without even knowing it. There was no pleasure in that."

"You're against addiction, then?"

"I'm against addiction to all things that are damaging and unnecessary."

"Like what?"

"Speed, comfort, violence, usury."

"You didn't mention drugs."

"Those, too. Legal drugs, too. And then there are some damaging things that are only necessary *because* we are addicted to them."

"For instance?"

"Petroleum. Most poisons. Automobiles."

"You're trying to change the subject, aren't you?"

"No, I'm just pointing to one of the dangers of the tobacco controversy."

"And what might that be?"

"That it is, to some extent, a red herring. In calling attention to the dangers of one kind of addiction, the tobacco controversy distracts from the much greater danger that we are an addictive society—that our people are rushing from one expensive and dangerous fix to another, from drugs to war to useless merchandise to various commercial thrills, and that our corporate pushers are addicted to our addictions."

"But say we are an addictive society, does that make the tobacco addiction right or excusable?"

"Of course not. It only means we ought to be aware of our inconsistency in condemning tobacco and excusing other damaging addictions, some of which are much more threatening than tobacco. Many people would like to think that our diseases are caused by one simple thing, like tobacco, which can be easily blamed on one group and fairly easily given up. But of course they are fooling themselves. One reason that people die of diseases is that they have grown old enough to die of something; they are mortal, a fact that modern humans don't like to face. Another reason is that as a people we live unhealthy lives. We breathe unhealthy air, drink unhealthy water, eat unhealthy food, eat too much, do no physical work, and so forth."

"But the question remains, how can you have quit smoking yourself because you recognize the danger and yet support the tobacco economy?"

"I don't support the tobacco economy, which involves much that I don't like—seductive advertising, for one thing. I support the tobacco program."

"What is that?"

"To risk oversimplification, it is an arrangement, sponsored by the federal government, voted for by the farmers, by which they agree to limit production in order to secure a livable return on investment and labor. This strategy of production control is commonplace in other productive industries but rare in farming. And the tobacco program has worked well. In my part of the country, it has ensured the survival of thousands of small farmers for more than half a century."

"Why should these people receive a government subsidy for growing a crop that the government acknowledges to be dangerous to health?"

"It is not a subsidy. The tobacco that receives a top

bid that is less than the support price is placed under loan by the program, the title to the crop remaining with the farmer until its ultimate sale by the cooperative. The government supplies the loan, which is repaid with interest and all expenses. And for several years now, tobacco farmers and manufacturers have been assessed one cent each per pound to pay administrative and other costs so that the program can be operated at no net cost to taxpayers."

"But it's tobacco they're growing. To support the program is to support tobacco and everything that goes with it."

"Well, let me ask *you* a question. Do you think everybody is going to quit smoking?"

"I suppose, considering the failure of Prohibition and the current popularity of illegal drugs, the answer probably is no."

"And there is a probability, isn't there, that condemnations and warnings, even proofs of danger, will make tobacco more attractive to some people?"

"Yes, I suppose so."

"And if some people continue to use it, other people will continue to grow it—is that not right?"

"I suppose it is."

"And so, if you destroyed the program, destroying in the process the farmers who depend on the program, who would grow the tobacco?"

"I haven't thought much about that. Large corporate growers under contract to the tobacco companies? Cheap laborers in Third World countries? I don't know."

"Most of the farmers who now grow it would, at any rate, be out of business."

"Probably."

"And what would become of them?"

"They could move to the city."

"And into other work?"

"Maybe."

"Or they could go on welfare?"

"Maybe."

"But you don't know. You do admit that whatever happened, the loss of the program would be extremely painful, disorienting, and costly for many thousands of families?"

"Yes, I will admit that."

"So, you see, to support the program is only to say that if tobacco is to be grown, you want it to be grown by the people who have always grown it—not by the sort for whom the failure of these people would be a 'window of opportunity.' "

"Now let me ask *you* something. If these people can't make it on their own, if they must always be helped by some sort of program or other, why not let them fail? Is that not the way things should be—and, in fact, are? Adapt or die. The survival of the fittest. If they can't survive, they deserve to fail. And, yes, their failure then properly becomes a 'window of opportunity' for somebody else."

"Well, I would question the historical validity of that idea and that attitude. I don't believe that any human community can be shown to have survived by the principle of all-out competition among its members, which the Bible (if that matters to you) explicitly forbids. And the implications for land use of that principle are absolutely ruinous. It makes impossible the establishment of a competent, long-lasting, soil-husbanding community on the land. Your 'fittest,' you know, would be the biggest or the wealthiest but not the best caretakers."

"The fact remains: you support the people who grow tobacco that supports an addiction you say you don't support."

"You bet I do! They are my own people, who are as good as other people."

"You can be a good person and grow tobacco?"

"Why don't you say what you really have in mind: Can you be a good person and be a sinner? Our religious tradition certainly says you can. People have faults and they have virtues. Which they have the most of is a judgment we are not supposed to make, for the very good reason that none of us can be sure of having all the evidence."

"But our religious tradition also warns us again and again of the danger of choosing a known evil over a known good."

"That's true. But for most tobacco farmers, the growing of tobacco has not been so clearly a moral choice. They did not choose to grow tobacco in the same sense that David chose to send Uriah into battle. Many of them began growing tobacco before the moral issue arose. They were simply born to the crop, as were the generations before them, going back to the seventeenth century. The younger ones—the ones born, say, after the surgeon general's report of 1964—were either born to tobacco growing or they bought into it when they bought their farms. For them, tobacco growing came, literally, with the territory. In tobacco country, the choice not to grow tobacco (in the circumstances of the present agricultural economy) is tantamount to a choice not to farm."

"And yet now they all know the argument against tobacco. Now it is an evil that they knowingly consent to."

"That is true. They consent to it in the same way that people involved in the present energy economy consent to a whole array of toxic exhausts and other results that they know to be evil. They consent, they are guilty, and they can't see their way out."

"You are going on as if you expect to win this argument. Do you?"

"Do I expect to argue my way to some uncontestable justification of tobacco growing? No. I am arguing only that tobacco growing is a complex, difficult issue. And I am explaining why I choose to stand with my people in their dilemma."

"In other words, why you don't dissociate yourself from this evil. Why don't you?"

"Why don't I dissociate myself from automobiles? Because I don't see how to do it—not yet. And I don't want to dissociate myself from the world."

"Well, I've heard you speak of some things—war, for instance, and the nuclear power industry, and the use of throwaway containers—as if you would like to see those evils stopped at once. Why not tobacco? If we can't stop people from using it, why don't we immediately put an end to any form of governmental approval of or support for its use?"

"Because that would destroy the program, which would destroy many farmers. There are alternatives, you know, to war, nuclear power, and throwaway containers."

"And tobacco farmers have no alternative to growing tobacco?"

"At present, none at all. That's why their 'choice'

to grow tobacco is not really a choice. They have had, as farmers, nothing else to choose."

"What sort of alternative do they need?"

"They need a crop, or several crops, that can produce a comparable income from comparable acreages, that can be grown with family and neighborhood labor, and for which there is a dependable market."

"They need to be growing food crops, you mean —fruits and vegetables."

"I think so. Along with the meat and milk that they already produce."

I see you are still clinging to the idea of an agricultural economy of diversified small farms that produce for local markets and local consumers."

"Yes, I'm still clinging to it. I want people to continue to eat. I want them to have, as dependably as possible, a local supply of good food. I want their food budget to support a thriving population of local farmers. That way, the land will thrive."

"And you see the tobacco farmers as necessary to that?"

"I see *all* farmers—all that are left and, I hope, some more—as necessary to that. Tobacco farmers are farmers and among the best of them; their know-how is a great public asset, if the public only recognized it. They are farming some very good land. They should be growing food for the people of their region, the people of neighboring cities—or they should have a viable choice of doing so. The people who so eagerly condemn them for growing tobacco should be just as eager to help them find alternative crops. It is wrong to condemn people for doing a thing and then offer no alternative but failure. A person could get mad about that."

"So you're not reconciled to your people's dependence on tobacco?"

"Far from it."

"You see it as a problem to be solved?"

"I see it as a problem to be solved. And that means, too, that I'm not reconciled to the general lack of interest in solving it."

"You mean that in state government and the universities there is no interest?"

"I would describe their interest, so far, as small— too small to generate any real hope of a solution. But the difficulties are enormous, and they had better be acknowledged. For one thing, the idea of local food economies, or 'local food self-sufficiency,' has few advocates and, so far as I know, no powerful ones; it has been eclipsed by the 'global economy' and the 'free market.' For another, most people are satisfied so far with the present system of food supply—though it is a satisfaction based on ignorance. And most difficult of all, if we are to wean farmers from tobacco onto other crops, we must somehow cause a local demand and a local supply to come into existence simultaneously."

"Do you foresee no help with this from the federal government?"

"The federal government sponsors the tobacco program, which is unusual behavior for the federal government, and the program has always had to deal with the dangers implicit in its unusualness. It has always had enemies, for in general the federal government's agricultural policy has been exactly the fight for survival that you were talking about: leave the markets unregulated and production uncontrolled, and let the farmers compete against each other year after year to survive the overproduction that is the result of their competition; then, every year, the 'least efficient' farmers fail, and their failure makes American agriculture stronger and better. The government, so to speak, sees homicide as the perfect cure—which it is, if you like homicide. Let me be plain with you. I see no chance at all that the federal government will soon take to heart the issue of the survival of tobacco farmers, or of any other farmers, or the survival of the rural communities those farmers represent. It would be pleasant to hope otherwise, but that would be to hope without reason. Nor do I hope for much from state governments or universities. The consensus seems to be that whoever or whatever fails deserves to fail and that something better will inevitably be built on such failures."

"You have, then, no hope?"

"To have given up illusory hope is not to be hopeless. I see, simply, that the institutions that have most influenced agriculture for the last forty or fifty years have demonstrated an almost perfect lack of interest in the survival of farmers."

"And so what hope do you have?"

"When hope leaves government, it must go to the people. So long as there is a demonstrable need and an imaginable answer, there is hope. We need to make it possible for farmers to choose not to grow tobacco and yet continue farming, and we need a better, safer, fresher supply of food, which is to say a *local* supply. And these two needs are, in fact, the same."

"You're going too fast. Why, necessarily, a *local* supply?"

"Well, the more local, the more fresh—there's no problem with that, is there?"

"No."

"And as you shorten the distance between consumer and producer, you increase the consumer's power to know and influence the quality of food. Kentucky consumers, for instance, could influence Kentucky farmers much more easily than they could influence California farmers."

"I can see that."

"Moreover, 'fresh' implies short distances and therefore lower expenditures for transportation, packaging, refrigeration, national advertising campaigns, and so on. A local food economy, in short, implies higher prices for farmers and lower costs to consumers."

"And you think the government doesn't see this but the people do?"

"Some people see it now. And more are going to see it, for it is going to become easier to see. And those who see it don't have to wait for the government to see it before they do something."

"But what can they do?"

"They can start buying produce from local farmers."

"As individuals?"

"As individuals, if necessary. But groups can do it, too, and can do it more effectively—conservation organizations, consumer groups, churches, local merchants, whoever is concerned. The government's approval is not necessary. In fact, the process has already begun. Scattered all over the country, there are farmers who are selling produce directly to urban consumers. There have been consumer cooperatives for this sort of dealing for a good many years. Local merchants sometimes stock local produce. If churches and conservation organizations—the two groups with most reason to be concerned—would get involved, much more could be accomplished. But everything that is done demonstrates a possibility and suggests more that might be done. That is the way it will grow."

"What are you talking about—some kind of revolution?"

"Not 'revolution.' I'm talking about economic secession—just quietly forming the means of withdrawal, not only from the tobacco economy but from the entire economy of exploitive land use that is ruining both the countryside and the country communities. The principle of this new economy would simply be good use—the possibility, often demonstrated, that land and people can be used without being destroyed. And this new economy would understand, first of all, that the ruin of farmers solves *no* problem and makes many."

—1991

PEACEABLENESS
TOWARD ENEMIES

Some Notes on the Gulf War

I. We went to war in the Middle East because our leaders believed that war was their only choice. If this war had been an issue only of the present time, as our leaders would like us to think, any discussion of its origins or effects would be pointless. But we know that this war descended from a history of war and that it evokes the fear of other wars that may descend from it. To ask, in the circumstances of that history and that fear, if war should have been the only choice is to imply no disrespect toward our country but merely to do one's duty as a citizen and a human being.

II. This latest war has been justified on a number of grounds: that it was a war to liberate Kuwait; that it was a war to defend "the civilized world" against a dangerous maniac; that it was a war to preserve peace; that it was a war to inaugurate a "new world order"; that it was a war to defend the American Way of Life; that it was a war to defend our supply of cheap oil. These justifications are not satisfactory, even when one supposes that they are sincerely believed.

III. What can we mean by the statement that we were "liberating" Kuwait? Kuwait was not a democratic nation. If it was imperative to "liberate" it after Saddam's invasion, why was it not equally imperative to "liberate" it before? And why is it not equally imperative to liberate Tibet or China, for instance, or any of the other nations under nondemocratic rule? In the Gulf War, we who are the children of a revolution against monarchy were fighting a dictator to "liberate" a monarchy; meanwhile, the former Soviet Union was suppressing, with little objection from us, an authentic movement for liberty in the Baltic nations.

IV. It may be true that Saddam Hussein is a dangerous madman. But this justification seriously embarrassed our claim to be able to control or limit the violence of the war. Madmen are by definition out of control, as Saddam Hussein's attacks on Israel and his release of oil into the Persian Gulf pretty well prove. In dealing with a madman, people of common sense try not to provoke him to greater acts of madness. How Saddam's acts of violence were to be satisfactorily limited or controlled by our own acts of greater violence has not been explained.

V. This war was said to be "about peace." So have they all been said to be. This was another in our series of wars "to end war." But peace is not the result of war, any more than love is the result of hate or generosity the result of greed. As a war in defense of peace, this one in the Middle East has failed, as all its predecessors have done. Like all its predecessors, it was the result of the failure, on the part of all of its participants, to be peaceable.

vi. If this was a war to bring about a "new world order," then we needed to deal with the fundamental incompatibility between order and victory —which we did not do. The contemplated "new world order" was presumably one to be presided over, enforced, and exploited by a newly victorious United States. But victory for some requires defeat for others. And those who have been defeated will not be satisfied for long with an order founded on their defeat. One such victory will sooner or later require another. In fact, this war produced not order but disorder probably greater than the disorder with which we began. We have by no means shown that disorder can be put in order by means of suffering, death, and destruction.

vii. One is constrained to believe, therefore, that this was a war in defense of the American Way of Life, a way of life that is dependent on cheap oil from the Middle East. What the war was "about" was power—military power fighting for the security of petroleum power and for the power, ease, and wealth that come from the exploitation of petroleum power.

viii. But we must also consider the possibility that this war happened not because we had a purpose in fighting it but simply because we were prepared for it, because we wanted to show what could be accomplished by our terrible new weapons, and because we "needed" just the sort of victory that we won. It is well understood that the mere possession of any piece of equipment is a powerful incentive to use it. Our aimlessness and apparent bewilderment in the aftermath of the war may be an indication that the war itself was virtually without a purpose.

IX. A number of things about our attitude toward this war were troubling, and the most troubling was our willingness to impose the whole burden of it on the young people in the military services and their families. We were evidently determined to preserve at all costs a way of life in which we will contemplate no restraints. We sent an enormous force of our young men and women to kill and to be killed in defense of our oil supply, but we have done nothing to conserve that supply or to reduce our dependence on it. We will not ration petroleum fuels. We will not mention the possibility of more taxes. We wish to give our people the impression that except for their children, nothing will be required of them.

X. About equally troubling is the tone of technological optimism that accompanied the war's beginning and that still surrounds it. The assumption on the part of the newspeople and evidently on the part of many of our politicians and military experts has been that this was a war of scientific precision and predictability, that we knew exactly what we were doing, what was involved, how long it would take, and what the results would be. Reporters' questions to the officials and generals were premised on the assumption that this "operation" was one in which somebody knew everything and was in control. There was a great deal of awed discussion of "smart bombs," "the weapons of tomorrow," and so on. Of course, anyone who uses tools can testify that results invariably become more complex and less predictable as force is increased. When our leaders talked about the results of this war, they were talking about victory and the political order that presumably would be imposed (for a while) by the victor. They were not talking about the deaths and griefs, the economic destructions, the intensified hatreds and resentments, the changed patterns of poverty and wealth, and the ecological damages that would also be results and that would not be readily predictable or controllable. The confession, by certain pro-war politicians, that some of the disorderly and lamentable results of the war were "not foreseen" was surely the war's most foreseeable result.

XI. Closely connected to this technological optimism is the renewed whistling in the dark of American nationalism. The war has been seized on as evidence that "America is not in decline." And there has been more talk of "the world's highest standard of living," "the world's biggest gross national product," "the world's most influential and powerful country." Much of this talk about our power and wealth is, of course, true, but it is also true that we are in decline. Our wealth is great, but our economy has been seriously damaged by the greed, selfishness, and shortsightedness that have become its ruling principles. Our power is great, but in spite of its vaunted precision, it is applied more and more ruthlessly and clumsily. We are increasingly making this a nation of peace, security, and freedom for the rich. We are at present completing the economic destruction of our rural and agricultural communities. We are destroying our farmlands, our forests, our water sources. We are polluting the air, the water, the land. We have almost done away with the private ownership of usable property and with small, private economic enterprises of all kinds. Our professions have become greedy, unscrupulous, and unaffordable. Our factory products are shoddy and overpriced.

If we are the most wealthy and powerful country in the world, we are also the most wasteful, both of nature and of humanity. This society is making life extremely difficult for the unwealthy and the unpowerful: children, old people, women (especially wives and mothers), country people, the poor, the unemployed, the homeless. We are failing in marriage and failing our family responsibilities. The number of single-parent households is increasing. Our children are ill raised and ill taught. We are trying—and predictably failing—to replace parenthood and home life with "day care" and with school. Our highways, shopping malls, nursing homes, and day-care centers are full; the homeless are everywhere in our streets; our homes are empty. We are suffering many kinds of damage from sexual promiscuity. We are addicted to drugs, to TV, and to gasoline. Violence is literally everywhere. While we waged war abroad, an undeclared civil war was being fought every day in our streets, our homes, our workplaces, and our classrooms.

And none of these problems can be corrected merely by wealth, power, and technology. The world's most powerful military force cannot help at all.

xii. The circumstances of this war made obscure such apparently simple questions as "Who is the enemy?" and "Whom is this war against?"

xiii. The enemy was said to be Iraq, or Iraq as ruled by Saddam Hussein. But in Iraq under the rule of Saddam Hussein, we faced an enemy who had been armed, fortified, equipped, trained, and encouraged by ourselves and our friends. Our government gave aid to Saddam Hussein, indulged his human rights abuses and his use of poison gas, and encouraged him to think that we would not oppose his ambitions. We sold him equipment that could be used to develop nuclear weapons, missiles, and poison gas. We sold him toxins and bacteria that could be used in biological warfare. If this was a war against a "foreign enemy," it was also a spasm of our own corporate and professional anarchy.

xiv. It was, as any war must be, in part a war against ourselves. Even in winning, we lost. Many of our young people were killed or hurt—though we look on this as a bargain price for the massive slaughter of our enemies. Our war industries are richer, but as a nation we are poorer. And though we have achieved "victory" by the damage that we did in the Middle East, we are poorer for that damage as well.

xv. It was not just Saddam Hussein's world that we damaged; it was *our* world. As every modern war had been and must be, this was a war against the world. In order to damage Saddam Hussein and his people, we damaged the earth. In order to protect himself and his people, Saddam Hussein damaged the earth. There was much talk in the press of Saddam Hussein's "crime" of releasing oil into the Persian Gulf. And yet we knew that he could and probably would do this; it was something we were willing to risk. It was the sort of thing that will inevitably happen in industrial warfare in industrial nations. Let us admit that the only solution to "world problems" that is in keeping with our military means is the destruction of the world.

xvi. A war against the world is helplessly a war against the people of the world. Against everybody. The innocent. The children. Increasingly, as modern militarism builds and brawls over the face of the planet, people of ordinary decency are thinking of the children. What about the children? we ask as our leaders acknowledge the inevitability of "some civilian casualties"—or "collateral casualties," as they put it. But we are thinking not just of the children who are living beneath the bombs. We are thinking, too, of our own children to whom someone must explain that some people—including some of "our" people—look on the deaths of children as an acceptable cost of victory.

xvii. There is no dodging the fact that war diminishes freedom. This war increased government secrecy (which is at any time a threat to freedom) and imposed government censorship of the press. And it increased governmental and popular pressure toward uniformity of thought and opinion. War always encourages a patriotism that means not love of country but unquestioning obedience to power. Freedom, of course, requires diversity of opinion. It not only tolerates political dissent but encourages and depends on it. Nevertheless, it was only to be expected that some of the voices calling for the "liberation" of Kuwait were also calling for censorship of the press and suppression of dissent in the United States.

xviii. We concluded in 1945, after our atomic bombing of Hiroshima and Nagasaki, that we had made war "unthinkable"—and we have gone on thinking of it, preparing for it, fighting it, suffering from it, and profiting from it ever since. But now, having completed our third major war since 1950, it does not seem at all farfetched to suggest that even so-called conventional war has become not only unthinkable but obsolete—for the reasons that I have given: that it is impossible to foresee or to limit its results; that in a "global economy," the designations of "enemy" and "friend" are increasingly difficult to define; that every industrial war is now a war against everybody and against the world; that children and other innocents are impossible to exempt from physical danger; that even wars fought "for freedom" diminish freedom. War is obsolete, in short, because it can no longer produce a net good, even to the winner.

xix. The concept of "righteous war," as our leaders should be aware, is certainly obsolete. Modern warfare is an absolute evil; it is Hell, as William Tecumseh Sherman rightly said. And it is impossible for leaders or nations to exempt themselves from that evil while using it. Any leader of a modern military power—whatever the allegations or proofs of the evil of the enemy—is a leader by virtue of his or her willingness to inflict unprecedented destruction and suffering on innocent humans, on innocent nonhuman creatures, and on the earth.

xx. But even if such a war could be righteous, it would still cost too much in lives, in ecological health, and in money to be affordable. History and our own experience inform us that we can expect to deal with tyrants, aggressors, and even madmen or madwomen with some frequency. It is obvious that we cannot frequently afford to send a massive military force to a battlefield thousands of miles from home.

xxi. If modern warfare is obsolete and unaffordable, then how could we have committed ourselves in the Middle East to the most modern of all wars? We did so, I would argue, because such a war is an implicit requirement of our ruling economic assumptions. This was a "free market" war—the result of bad foreign policy that was, in turn, the result of bad domestic policy.

xxii. The "free market" theory holds that the use and distribution of the material goods of the earth should be determined exclusively by economics. It holds that all that is needed in order to have a sufficiency of goods is purchasing power. It discards any idea of local or national self-sufficiency in favor of a "world market," free of obstructions to international purchasing power. It proposes that no nation should protect or promote its domestic economy for the sake of self-sufficiency or independence. This is our government's aim in its continuing effort to revise the General Agreement on Tariffs and Trade so as to remove all local and national programs affecting agricultural production. The assumption is that we, as a nation, do not need to produce, or conserve, or use well, or protect the source of anything we need; money alone will determine the availability of goods. A further assumption is that a nation can generate sufficient purchasing power indefinitely, without a thriving, highly diversified domestic economy. The "free market" theorists assume, in short, that an adequate national economy may be composed of many consumers, few producers, and even fewer rich manipulators at the top. This theory attributes a kind of creative or magical power to money that money does not have, and that is dangerous enough. But it also and more dangerously involves an inevitable, large-scale dependence on foreign supplies.

xxiii. Under the rule of the "free market" ideology, we have gone through two decades of an energy crisis without an effective energy policy. Because of an easy and thoughtless reliance on imported oil, we have no adequate policy for the conservation of gasoline and other petroleum products. We have no adequate policy for the development or use of other, less harmful forms of energy. We have no adequate system of public transportation. We fought Saddam Hussein because our willing dependence on foreign energy had put us helplessly under his influence. Having defeated him in war, we are still under his influence, for what we have done to defeat him will continue to affect us, and inevitably for the worst.

But we must pay whatever price is demanded in blood, in ecological damage, and in money (or debt), because we are helpless to provide for ourselves what must be provided for us by suppliers in the Middle East and elsewhere.

xxiv. This neglect of domestic economy applies not just to energy but to all necessities. We are destroying our farms and farm communities, for example, keeping costs high and incomes low, for the sake of "competitiveness on the world market." The proposed revisions of the General Agreement on Tariffs and Trade would throw our farmers into competition with farmers of the Third World, thereby endangering agricultural economies both here and there. We are destroying our forests in the same way. We have allowed vital industries here to be destroyed by the importation of cheap goods from abroad. For example, we are now importing 59 percent of our textiles and clothing. Having just finished an oil war, we may expect sooner or later to be involved in a textile war, a food war—or a war over *anything* that we need but cannot provide.

xxv. We were encouraging and protecting Saddam Hussein virtually until the day we went to war against him, partly because we needed his oil and we needed Iraq as a market for our agricultural commodities and manufactured goods. But this generous help to Saddam Hussein, our enemy-to-be, was by no means the first contradiction in which "free market" or "global" economics has involved us. Only a few years ago, for example, we were exerting ourselves mightily to sell American grain to the Soviet Union, our then-enemy whom we were armed to annihilate. This sort of thing is absurd, of course, but the absurdity is visible only to common sense. The apparent inconsistency is resolved by the concept that food and arms are equally and indifferently commodities in the "global economy." The internationalists of trade (American and otherwise) are happy to sell wheat or arms to either side of any conflict. The real conflict at any given moment, then, is not primarily that between nations, or even that between the world economy and the national interests, but that between the world economy and the world.

XXVI. We have witnessed the development, since World War II, of a national economy that is not at all related to the prosperity of American localities and communities. As the nation has prospered, the country has declined. Worse, we have seen the emergence into power in this country of an economic elite who have invested their lives and loyalties in no locality and in no nation, whose ambitions are global, and who are so insulated by wealth and power that they feel no need to care about what happens to any place. Their economic globalism follows closely the pattern of the economic nationalism of the industrialists who have so brutally exploited the Appalachian coal fields. The global industrialists will go anywhere and destroy anything, so long as there is a market for the result. Under their "leadership," we are squandering our domestic economy in order to plunder foreign economies. This is the purpose of the "free market" and the proposed revisions of the General Agreement on Tariffs and Trade.

xxvii. The Gulf War, our latest failure to be peaceable, was thus linked to a much larger failure: the failure of those who most profit from the world to be able to imagine the world except in terms of abstract quantities. They cannot imagine any part of the world or any human community in any part of the world as separate in any way from issues of monetary profit.

xxviii. Modern war and modern industry are much alike, not just in their technology and methodology but also in this failure of imagination. It is no accident that they cause similar devastations. There can be little doubt that industrial disfigurements of nature and industrial diminishments of human beings prepare the souls of nations for industrial war in which places become "enemy territory," people become "targets" or "collateral casualties," and bombing sorties become "turkey shoots."

xxix. If, in this war, we were defending "civilization," as we claimed, then we were proposing a more difficult criticism of our civilization than we have so far been willing to make. Not all of "civilization" and its works are defensible. History leaves no doubt that most of the most regrettable crimes committed by human beings have been committed by those human beings who thought of themselves as "civilized." What, we must ask, does our civilization possess that is worth defending?

xxx. One thing worth defending, I suggest, is the imperative to imagine the lives of beings who are not ourselves and are not like ourselves: animals, plants, gods, spirits, people of other countries and other races, people of the other sex, places—and enemies. To mention only the earliest instance, the most attractive hero of the *Iliad* is not Greek but Trojan: Hector, a good man, a good family man, a good friend. It is over the body of Hector that Greek anger finally gives way to compassion.

xxxi. Another precious possession of our culture is the idea that human lives matter individually and ultimately. This idea, which is ancient in religion and in art, began to flower politically only two hundred fifteen years ago in the declaration that "all men are created equal" and "endowed by their Creator with certain unalienable Rights." They were not held to be equal in nature or in fortune but to possess equally the right to live, to be free, and to try to be happy. Suddenly it was imaginable that a government should respect these rights as belonging to "*all* men." We know that this is an idea of great force, and we have changed it only by making it more inclusive.

xxxii. By "all men" we now mean "all the people of the United States." It may be that this idea is so potent that it will someday require all governments to respect the individual lives and rights of all the people of the world. I hope so. But must we not ask *how* this precious idea can be defended abroad or preserved at home by people encouraged to forget that the enemy they are about to kill is a human being?

xxxiii. Perhaps the most depressing development of this latest war is the idea, creeping into editorials and commentaries, that war is inevitable, that it will be inescapably a part of our national life as long as we are a nation, and that we can continue to be a nation only by war. We must be prepared to fight on and on, for we will inevitably meet competitors who will become enemies, and some of these enemies will be madmen or madwomen. Surely it is too soon to come to such a desperate conclusion, for there is one great possibility that we have hardly tried: that we can come to peace by being peaceable.

xxxiv. That possibility, though little honored, is well known; its most famous statement is this: "Love your enemies, bless them that curse you, do good to them that hate you, and pray for them which despitefully use you and persecute you." I did not include this idea as a precious possession of our civilization because it is not one. It is an idea given to our civilization but so far not accepted.

xxxv. In times of war, our leaders always speak of their prayers. They wish us to know that they say prayers because they wish us to believe that they are deeply worried and that they take their responsibilities seriously. Perhaps they believe or hope that prayer will help. But within the circumstances of war, *prayer* becomes a word as befuddled in meaning as *liberate* or *order* or *victory* or *peace*. These prayers are usually understood to be Christian prayers. But Christian prayers are made to or in the name of Jesus, who loved, prayed for, and forgave his enemies and who instructed his followers to do likewise. A Christian supplicant, therefore, who has resolved to kill those whom he is enjoined to love, to bless, to do good to, to pray for, and to forgive as he hopes to be forgiven is not conceivably in a situation in which he can be at peace with himself. Anyone who has tried to apply this doctrine to a merely personal enmity will be aware of the enormous anguish that it could cause a national leader in wartime. No wonder that national leaders have ignored it for nearly two thousand years.

xxxvi. We have made much of Saddam's tyranny, which logically would imply some sympathy for his people, who were the first victims of his tyranny. But we have shown them no sympathy at all, have regarded them not even as human beings but as "fish in a barrel" or as the targets in a "turkey shoot." Having killed thousands on thousands of them, virtually without seeing or thinking of them, we have hardly spared for them a word of regret or for their families a word of sympathy. In fact, we have no sympathy for them. For our leaders and much of our public, the appalling statistics of death and suffering in Iraq merely prove the efficiency of our military technology. Ignoring the Gospels' command to be merciful, forgiving, loving, and peaceable, our leaders have prayed only for the success of their arms and policies and have thus made for themselves a state religion—exactly what they claim to fear in "fundamentalist" Islam. But why God might particularly favor a nation whose economy is founded foursquare on the seven deadly sins is a mystery that has not been explained.

xxxvii. The idea of peaceableness toward enemies is a religious principle. Whether or not it could be believed, much less practiced, apart from authentic religious faith, I do not know. I can only point out that the idea of the ultimate importance of individual lives is also a religious principle and that it finally became a political principle of significant power and influence.

xxxviii. Peaceableness toward enemies is an idea that will, of course, continue to be denounced as impractical. It has been too little tried by individuals, much less by nations. It will not readily or easily serve those who are greedy for power. It cannot be effectively used for bad ends. It could not be used as the basis of an empire. It does not afford opportunities for profit. It involves danger to practitioners. It requires sacrifice. And yet it seems to me that it *is* practical, for it offers the only escape from the logic of retribution. It is the only way by which we can cease to look to war for peace.

xxxix. Let us hasten to the question that apologists for killing always ask: If somebody raped or murdered a member of my family, would I not want to kill him? Of course I would, and I daresay I would enjoy killing him. Or her. If asked, however, if I think that it would do any good, I must reply that I do not. The logic of retribution implies no end and no hope. If I kill my enemy, and his brother kills me, and my brother kills his brother, and so on and on, we may all have strong motives and even good reasons; the world may be better off without all of us. And yet this is a form of behavior that we have wisely outlawed. We have outlawed it, that is, in private life. In our national life, it remains the established and honored procedure.

xl. The essential point is the ancient one: that to be peaceable is, by definition, to be peaceable in time of conflict. Peaceableness is not the amity that exists between people who agree, nor is it the exhaustion or jubilation that follows war. It is not passive. It is the ability to act to resolve conflict without violence. If it is not a practical and a practicable method, it is nothing. As a practicable method, it reduces helplessness in the face of conflict. In the face of conflict, the peaceable person may find several solutions, the violent person only one.

XLI. We seem to be following, on the one hand, the logic of preventive war, according to which we probably ought to kill all heads of state and their supporters to keep them from sooner or later becoming power-hungry maniacs who will force us to fight a *big* war to save freedom, civilization, peace, gentleness, and brotherly love. On the other hand, we have our customary practice of aiding, encouraging, and winking at power-hungry maniacs, because we think them useful and secretly admire them, until they become strong enough to threaten *our* power-hungry maniacs. But peaceableness is not the same thing as this planning for war and making war, or this reckless dealing in power. If it is to mean anything, peaceableness has to operate all the time, not lie dormant until the emergence of power-hungry maniacs. Amish pacifism makes sense because the Amish are peaceable all the time. If they attacked their neighbors and then, when their neighbors retaliated, started loving them, praying for them, and turning the other cheek, they would be both wrong and stupid. Of course, as the Amish know, peaceableness can get you killed. I suppose they would reply that war can get you killed, too, and is more likely to get you killed than peaceableness—and also that when a peaceable person is killed, peaceableness survives.

xlii. As it is true that we are now helplessly dependent on foreign supplies, it is also true that we are helplessly dependent on military force. We believe, we say, in diplomacy, but only in diplomacy backed by military force. We believe, we say, in sanctions, but only in sanctions quickly replaced by military force. Once the weapons are in place, the belligerent demands laid down, and the threats made, then neither side has more than two choices: fight or yield. Neither choice is attractive. But the fact, apparently, is that we don't understand anything but force because we have not tried to understand anything but force. Our approach to life in this world—in the use of our own land, as well as in dealing with foreign enemies—has been "massive force relentlessly applied."

xliii. At the same time, we undoubtedly long for peace. We would not be human if we did not. We long for peace, and we trust in war. No one can ignore the likelihood that modern war, because it is profitable and serves power, will continue until it destroys its own possibility, not by bringing peace but by destroying civilizaiton or the world, either slowly or quickly. But we must see, too, that such a prospect calls seriously into question the value of that "human intelligence" that we are so famous with ourselves for having.

xliv. If I put up many signs on my property, saying that I will shoot all trespassers, then I greatly in-

crease the possibility of two bad outcomes: that I
will eventually have to shoot a trespasser or that a
determined trespasser will come armed and shoot
me. If I want to forestall such possibilities, and at
the same time protect myself, then I will have to
do much more than withdraw my threat. I must
change my relationship to all potential trespassers.
I must be a good neighbor to my neighbors, not
out of fear, but in recognition both of our mutual
advantages and of the possibility that I may like
them. If all else fails, I must think of ways to make
my point and protect myself and my place without
destroying myself or my neighbors, my place or my
neighbors' places. This, of course, would not be
easy—but, then, neither would the alternative.

XLV. Those who would like to believe in progress
must be startled to realize that in the half century
between Hitler and Hussein our method of dealing
with belligerent madmen has not changed; *all* the
progress has been in the manufacturing of more and
more terrible weapons. And so we have still ahead
of us the most daunting question that humans have
ever had to ask: What can we do if, or when, we
are confronted by a madman who has a nuclear
bomb? We have no acceptable answer to that question, because the logic of war can lead to no acceptable answer. The logic of war, as we already
know, can produce only the idea of a "preemptive
strike"—a madman's idea—which would destroy
the world or a considerable part of it in order to
prevent the other madman from doing the same
thing with his bomb. And this leads to another
question that is merely absurd: What would be the

net good, to anybody, of doing that? Military logic
is thus driving us along an ever-narrowing gamut
of possibilities toward absurity, hopelessness, and
ruin.

XLVI. This appears to be a sufficient reason to ask
whether the logic of peaceableness is fundamentally
different from the logic of war. We must begin to
consider the possibility that the real agenda of
peaceableness is not at all the same as the agenda
of war or military defense, and in some respects it
is not the same as the agenda of politics. It would
be different from the military agenda because it
would look toward settlements and accommoda-
tions not ruled by the concepts of victory and defeat.
It would be to some extent different from the political agenda because it is unlikely to be advocated
at first by any political leader and because it must
rest on the changed lives and economies of individuals, families, and neighborhoods. What, then,
might be the agenda of peaceableness?

XLVII. We must recognize, first, that we have made
such progress in the technology of war that we have
destroyed the capacity of war to improve anything.
The Gulf War, typically, destroyed a large quantity
of the oil we were fighting to save.

XLVIII. And then we must recognize that peaceabil-
ity, as a way of dealing with large conflicts, is not
a dream but a proven possibility. We have the examples of Gandhi and Martin Luther King. We
have the histories of the Quakers, the Amish, and
other nonviolent sects and groups. We have the examples of some nations that have successfully pur-

sued policies of peaceableness over long stretches of time.

xlix. Third, we must give the same status and prestige to the virtues and the means of peaceableness as we have heretofore given to the means of war. We should, for a start, establish a peace academy that would have the same prestige and standing as the military academies have.

l. Fourth, we must recognize that the standards of the industrial economy lead inevitably to war against humans just as they lead inevitably to war against nature. We must learn to prefer quality over quantity, service over profit, neighborliness over competition, people and other creatures over machines, health over wealth, a democratic prosperity over centralized wealth and power, economic health over "economic growth."

li. Fifth, we must see that a nation cannot hope to live at peace without a domestic economy that is sound, diversified, decentralized, democratic, locally adapted, ecologically responsible, and reasonably self-sufficient.

lii. Sixth, if we are to have such an economy, we must repair our country and our society. We must stop the ruin of our forests and fields, waterways and seacoasts. We must end waste and pollution. We must renew our urban and rural communities. We must remake family life and neighborhood. We must reduce indebtedness, poverty, homelessness, violence. We must renew the possibility of a democratic distribution of usable property. We must take proper care of our children. We must quit treating them as commodities for the "job market" and teach them to be good neighbors and citizens and to do good work.

LIII. Finally, if we want to be at peace, we will have to waste less, spend less, use less, want less, need less. The most alarming sign of the state of our society now is that our leaders have the courage to sacrifice the lives of young people in war but have not the courage to tell us that we must be less greedy and less wasteful.

—1991

CHRISTIANITY
AND THE SURVIVAL
OF CREATION*

I

I confess that I have not invariably been comfortable in front of a pulpit; I have never been comfortable behind one. To be behind a pulpit is always a forcible reminder to me that I am an essayist and, in many ways, a dissenter. An essayist is, literally, a writer who attempts to tell the truth. Preachers must resign themselves to being either right or wrong; an essayist, when proved wrong, may claim to have been "just practicing." An essayist is privileged to speak without institutional authorization. A dissenter, of course, must speak without privilege.

I want to begin with a problem: namely, that the culpability of Christianity in the destruction of the natural world and the uselessness of Christianity in any effort to correct that destruction are now established

---

* This essay was delivered as a lecture at the Southern Baptist Theological Seminary in Louisville, Kentucky.

clichés of the conservation movement. This is a problem for two reasons.

First, the indictment of Christianity by the anti-Christian conservationists is, in many respects, just. For instance, the complicity of Christian priests, preachers, and missionaries in the cultural destruction and the economic exploitation of the primary peoples of the Western Hemisphere, as of traditional cultures around the world, is notorious. Throughout the five hundred years since Columbus's first landfall in the Bahamas, the evangelist has walked beside the conqueror and the merchant, too often blandly assuming that their causes were the same. Christian organizations, to this day, remain largely indifferent to the rape and plunder of the world and of its traditional cultures. It is hardly too much to say that most Christian organizations are as happily indifferent to the ecological, cultural, and religious implications of industrial economics as are most industrial organizations. The certified Christian seems just as likely as anyone else to join the military-industrial conspiracy to murder Creation.

The conservationist indictment of Christianity is a problem, second, because, however just it may be, it does not come from an adequate understanding of the Bible and the cultural traditions that descend from the Bible. The anti-Christian conservationists characteristically deal with the Bible by waving it off. And this dismissal conceals, as such dismissals are apt to do, an ignorance that invalidates it. The Bible is an inspired book written by human hands; as such, it is certainly subject to criticism. But the anti-Christian environmentalists have not mastered the first rule of the criticism of books: you have to read them before you criticize them. Our predicament now, I believe, requires us to learn to read and understand the Bible in the light of the present fact of Creation. This would seem to be a requirement both for Christians and for everyone concerned, but it entails a long work of true criticism—that is, of careful and judicious study, not dismissal. It entails, furthermore, the making of very precise distinctions between biblical instruction and the behavior of those peoples supposed to have been biblically instructed.

I cannot pretend, obviously, to have made so meticulous a study; even if I were capable of it, I would not live long enough to do it. But I have attempted to read the Bible with these issues in mind, and I see some virtually catastrophic discrepancies between biblical instruction and Christian behavior. I don't mean disreputable Christian behavior, either. The discrepancies I see are between biblical instruction and allegedly respectable Christian behavior.

If because of these discrepancies Christianity were dismissible, there would, of course, be no problem. We could simply dismiss it, along with the twenty centuries of unsatisfactory history attached to it, and start setting things to rights. The problem emerges only when we ask, Where then would we turn for instruction? We might, let us suppose, turn to another religion—a recourse that is sometimes suggested by the anti-Christian conservationists. Buddhism, for example, is certainly a religion that could guide us toward a right respect for the natural world, our fellow humans, and our fellow creatures. I owe a considerable debt myself to Buddhism and Buddhists. But there are an enormous number of people—and I am one of them—whose native religion, for better or worse, is Christianity. We were born to it; we began to learn about it before we became conscious; it is, whatever we think of it, an intimate belonging of our being; it informs our consciousness, our language, and our dreams. We can turn away from it or against it, but that will only bind us tightly to a reduced version of it. A better possibility is that this, our native religion, should survive and renew itself so that it may become as largely and truly instructive as we need it to be. On such a survival and renewal of the Christian religion may depend the survival of the Creation that is its subject.

II

If we read the Bible, keeping in mind the desirability of those two survivals—of Christianity and the Creation—we are apt to discover several things about which modern Christian organizations have kept remarkably quiet or to which they have paid little attention.

We will discover that we humans do not own the world or any part of it: "The earth is the Lord's, and the fulness thereof: the world and they that dwell therein."[1] There is in our human law, undeniably, the concept and right of "land ownership." But this, I think, is merely an expedient to safeguard the mutual belonging of people and places without which there can be no lasting and conserving human communities. This right of human ownership is limited by mortality and by natural constraints on human attention and responsibility; it quickly becomes abusive when used to justify large accumulations of "real estate," and perhaps for that reason such large accumulations are forbidden in the twenty-fifth chapter of Leviticus. In biblical terms, the "landowner" is the guest and steward of God: "The land is mine; for ye are strangers and sojourners with me."[2]

We will discover that God made not only the parts of Creation that we humans understand and approve but all of it: "All things were made by him; and without him was not anything made that was made."[3] And so we must credit God with the making of biting and stinging insects, poisonous serpents, weeds, poisonous weeds, dangerous beasts, and disease-causing microorganisms. That we may disapprove of these things does not mean that God is in error or that He ceded some of the work of Creation to Satan; it means that we are deficient in wholeness, harmony, and understanding—that is, we are "fallen."

We will discover that God found the world, as He made it, to be good, that He made it for His pleasure, and that He continues to love it and to find it worthy, despite its reduction and corruption by us. People who quote John 3:16 as an easy formula for getting to Heaven neglect to see the great difficulty implied in the statement that the advent of Christ was made possible by God's love for the world—not God's love for Heaven or for the world as it might be but for the world as it was and is. Belief in Christ is thus dependent on prior belief in the inherent goodness—the lovability—of the world.

We will discover that the Creation is not in any sense independent of the Creator, the result of a primal creative act long over and done with, but is the continuous, constant participation of all creatures in the being of God. Elihu said to Job that if God "gather unto himself his spirit and his breath; all flesh shall perish together."[4] And Psalm 104 says, "Thou sendest forth thy spirit, they are created." Creation is thus God's presence in creatures. The Greek Orthodox theologian Philip Sherrard has written that "Creation is nothing less than the manifestation of God's hidden Being."[5] This means that we and all other creatures live by a sanctity that is inexpressibly intimate, for to every creature, the gift of life is a portion of the breath and spirit of God. As the poet George Herbert put it:

> Thou art in small things great, not small in any . . .
> For thou art infinite in one and all.[6]

We will discover that for these reasons our destruction of nature is not just bad stewardship, or stupid economics, or a betrayal of family responsibility; it is the most horrid blasphemy. It is flinging God's gifts into His face, as if they were of no worth beyond that assigned to them by our destruction of them. To Dante, "despising Nature and her goodness" was a violence against God.[7] We have no entitlement from the Bible to exterminate or permanently destroy or hold in contempt anything on the earth or in the heavens above it or in the waters beneath it. We have the right to use the gifts of nature but not to ruin or waste them. We have the right to use what we need but no more, which is why the Bible forbids usury and great accumulations of property. The usurer, Dante said, "condemns Nature . . . for he puts his hope elsewhere."[8]

William Blake was biblically correct, then, when he said that "everything that lives is holy."[9] And Blake's great commentator Kathleen Raine was correct both biblically and historically when she said that "the sense of the holiness of life is the human norm."[10]

The Bible leaves no doubt at all about the sanctity

of the act of world-making, or of the world that was made, or of creaturely or bodily life in this world. We are holy creatures living among other holy creatures in a world that is holy. Some people know this, and some do not. Nobody, of course, knows it all the time. But what keeps it from being far better known than it is? Why is it apparently unknown to millions of professed students of the Bible? How can modern Christianity have so solemnly folded its hands while so much of the work of God was and is being destroyed?

III

Obviously, "the sense of the holiness of life" is not compatible with an exploitive economy. You cannot know that life is holy if you are content to live from economic practices that daily destroy life and diminish its possibility. And many if not most Christian organizations now appear to be perfectly at peace with the military-industrial economy and its "scientific" destruction of life. Surely, if we are to remain free and if we are to remain true to our religious inheritance, we must maintain a separation between church and state. But if we are to maintain any sense or coherence or meaning in our lives, we cannot tolerate the present utter disconnection between religion and economy. By "economy" I do not mean "economics," which is the study of money-making, but rather the ways of human housekeeping, the ways by which the human household is situated and maintained within the household of nature. To be uninterested in economy is to be uninterested in the practice of religion; it is to be uninterested in culture and in character. Probably the most urgent question

now faced by people who would adhere to the Bible is
this: What sort of economy would be responsible to the
holiness of life? What, for Christians, would be the
economy, the practices and the restraints, of "right live-
lihood"? I do not believe that organized Christianity
now has any idea. I think its idea of a Christian economy
is no more or less than the industrial economy—which
is an economy firmly founded on the seven deadly sins
and the breaking of all ten of the Ten Commandments.
Obviously, if Christianity is going to survive as more
than a respecter and comforter of profitable iniquities,
then Christians, regardless of their organizations, are
going to have to interest themselves in economy—which
is to say, in nature and in work. They are going to have
to give workable answers to those who say we cannot
live without this economy that is destroying us and our
world, who see the murder of Creation as the only way
of life.

The holiness of life is obscured to modern Christians also by the idea that the only holy place is the
built church. This idea may be more taken for granted
than taught; nevertheless, Christians are encouraged
from childhood to think of the church building as "God's
house," and most of them could think of their houses
or farms or shops or factories as holy places only with
great effort and embarrassment. It is understandably
difficult for modern Americans to think of their dwellings and workplaces as holy, because most of these are,
in fact, places of desecration, deeply involved in the
ruin of Creation.

The idea of the exclusive holiness of church build-
ings is, of course, wildly incompatible with the idea,
which the churches also teach, that God is present in
all places to hear prayers. It is incompatible with Scrip-

ture. The idea that a human artifact could contain or confine God was explicitly repudiated by Solomon in his prayer at the dedication of the Temple: "Behold, the heaven and the heaven of heavens cannot contain thee: how much less this house that I have builded?"[11] And these words of Solomon were remembered a thousand years later by Saint Paul, preaching at Athens:

> *God that made the world and all things therein, seeing that he is lord of heaven and earth, dwelleth not in temples made with hands . . .*
>
> *For in him we live, and move, and have our being; as certain also of your own poets have said.*[12]

Idolatry always reduces to the worship of something "made with hands," something confined within the terms of human work and human comprehension. Thus, Solomon and Saint Paul both insisted on the largeness and the at-largeness of God, setting Him free, so to speak, from *ideas* about Him. He is not to be fenced in, under human control, like some domestic creature; He is the wildest being in existence. The presence of His spirit in us is our wildness, our oneness with the wilderness of Creation. That is why subduing the things of nature to human purposes is so dangerous and why it so often results in evil, in separation and desecration. It is why the poets of our tradition so often have given nature the role not only of mother or grandmother but of the highest earthly teacher and judge, a figure of mystery and great power. Jesus' own specifications for his church have nothing at all to do with masonry and carpentry but only with people; his church is "where two or three are gathered together in my name."[13]

The Bible gives exhaustive (and sometimes exhausting) attention to the organization of religion: the building and rebuilding of the Temple; its furnishings; the orders, duties, and paraphernalia of the priesthood; the orders of rituals and ceremonies. But that does not disguise the fact that the most significant religious events recounted in the Bible do not occur in "temples made with hands." The most important religion in that book is unorganized and is sometimes profoundly disruptive of organization. From Abraham to Jesus, the most important people are not priests but shepherds, soldiers, property owners, workers, housewives, queens and kings, manservants and maidservants, fishermen, prisoners, whores, even bureaucrats. The great visionary encounters did not take place in temples but in sheep pastures, in the desert, in the wilderness, on mountains, on the shores of rivers and the sea, in the middle of the sea, in prisons. And however strenuously the divine voice prescribed rites and observances, it just as strenuously repudiated them when they were taken to be religion:

> *Your new moons and your appointed feasts my soul hateth: they are a trouble unto me; I am weary to bear them.*
>
> *And when you spread forth your hands, I will hide mine eyes from you: yea, when you make many prayers, I will not hear: your hands are full of blood.*
>
> *Wash you, make you clean; put away the evil of your doings from before mine eyes; cease to do evil;*
>
> *Learn to do well; seek judgment, relieve the oppressed, judge the fatherless, plead for the widow.*[14]

Religion, according to this view, is less to be celebrated in rituals than practiced in the world.

I don't think it is enough appreciated how much an outdoor book the Bible is. It is a "hypaethral book," such as Thoreau talked about—a book open to the sky. It is best read and understood outdoors, and the farther outdoors the better. Or that has been my experience of it. Passages that within walls seem improbable or incredible, outdoors seem merely natural. This is because outdoors we are confronted everywhere with wonders; we see that the miraculous is not extraordinary but the common mode of existence. It is our daily bread. Whoever really has considered the lilies of the field or the birds of the air and pondered the improbability of their existence in this warm world within the cold and empty stellar distances will hardly balk at the turning of water into wine—which was, after all, a very small miracle. We forget the greater and still continuing miracle by which water (with soil and sunlight) is turned into grapes.

It is clearly impossible to assign holiness exclusively to the built church without denying holiness to the rest of Creation, which is then said to be "secular." The world, which God looked at and found entirely good, we find none too good to pollute entirely and destroy piecemeal. The church, then, becomes a kind of preserve of "holiness," from which certified lovers of God assault and plunder the "secular" earth.

Not only does this repudiate God's approval of His work; it refuses also to honor the Bible's explicit instruction to regard the works of the Creation as God's revelation of Himself. The assignation of holiness exclusively to the built church is therefore logically accompanied by the assignation of revelation exclusively to the Bible. But Psalm 19 begins, "The heavens declare the glory of God; and the firmament sheweth his handiwork." The word of God has been revealed in facts from the moment of the third verse of the first chapter of Genesis: "Let there be light: and there was light." And Saint Paul states the rule: "The invisible things of him from the creation of the world are clearly seen, being understood by the things that are made."[15] Yet from this free, generous, and sensible view of things, we come to the idolatry of the book: the idea that nothing is true that cannot be (and has not been already) written. The misuse of the Bible thus logically accompanies the abuse of nature: if you are going to destroy creatures without respect, you will want to reduce them to "materiality"; you will want to deny that there is spirit or truth in them, just as you will want to believe that the only holy creatures, the only creatures with souls, are humans—or even only Christian humans.

By denying spirit and truth to the nonhuman Creation, modern proponents of religion have legitimized a form of blasphemy without which the nature- and culture-destroying machinery of the industrial economy could not have been built—that is, they have legitimized bad work. Good human work honors God's work. Good work uses no thing without respect, both for what it is in itself and for its origin. It uses neither tool nor material that it does not respect and that it does not love. It honors nature as a great mystery and power, as an indispensable teacher, and as the inescapable judge of all work of human hands. It does not dissociate life and work, or pleasure and work, or love and work, or usefulness and beauty. To work without pleasure or affection, to make a product that is not both useful and beautiful, is to dishonor God, nature, the thing that is made, and whomever it is made for. This is blasphemy: to make shoddy work of the work of God. But such blasphemy is not possible when the entire Creation is understood as holy and when the works of God are understood as embodying and thus revealing His spirit.

In the Bible we find none of the industrialist's contempt or hatred for nature. We find, instead, a poetry of awe and reverence and profound cherishing, as in these verses from Moses' valedictory blessing of the twelve tribes:

> *And of Joseph he said, Blessed of the Lord be his land, for the precious things of heaven, for the dew, and for the deep that croucheth beneath,*
> *And for the precious fruits brought forth by the sun, and for the precious things put forth by the moon,*
> *And for the chief things of the ancient mountains, and for the precious things of the lasting hills,*
> *And for the precious things of the earth and fullness thereof, and for the good will of him that dwelt in the bush.*[16]

IV

I have been talking, of course, about a dualism that manifests itself in several ways: as a cleavage, a radical discontinuity, between Creator and creature, spirit and matter, religion and nature, religion and economy, worship and work, and so on. This dualism, I think, is the most destructive disease that afflicts us. In its best-known, its most dangerous, and perhaps its fundamental version, it is the dualism of body and soul. This is an issue as difficult as it is important, and so to deal with it we should start at the beginning.

The crucial test is probably Genesis 2:7, which

gives the process by which Adam was created: "The Lord God formed man of the dust of the ground, and breathed into his nostrils the breath of life: and man became a living soul." My mind, like most people's, has been deeply influenced by dualism, and I can see how dualistic minds deal with this verse. They conclude that the formula for man-making is man = body + soul. But that conclusion cannot be derived, except by violence, from Genesis 2:7, which is not dualistic. The formula given in Genesis 2:7 is not man = body + soul; the formula there is soul = dust + breath. According to this verse, God did not make a body and put a soul into it, like a letter into an envelope. He formed man of dust; then, by breathing His breath into it, He made the dust live. The dust, formed as man and made to live, did not *embody* a soul; it *became* a soul. "Soul" here refers to the whole creature. Humanity is thus presented to us, in Adam, not as a creature of two discrete parts temporarily glued together but as a single mystery.

We can see how easy it is to fall into the dualism of body and soul when talking about the inescapable worldly dualities of good and evil or time and eternity. And we can see how easy it is, when Jesus asks, "For what is a man profited, if he shall gain the whole world, and lose his own soul?"[17] to assume that he is condemning the world and appreciating the disembodied soul. But if we give to "soul" here the sense that it has in Genesis 2:7, we see that he is doing no such thing. He is warning that in pursuit of so-called material possessions, we can lose our understanding of ourselves as "living souls"—that is, as creatures of God, members of the holy community of Creation. We can lose the possibility of the atonement of that membership. For we are free, if we choose, to make a duality of our one living soul by disowning the breath of God that is our fundamental bond with one another and with other creatures.

But we can make the same duality by disowning the dust. The breath of God is only one of the divine gifts that make us living souls; the other is the dust. Most of our modern troubles come from our misunderstanding and misvaluation of this dust. Forgetting that the dust, too, is a creature of the Creator, made by the sending forth of His spirit, we have presumed to decide that the dust is "low." We have presumed to say that we are made of two parts: a body and a soul, the body being "low" because made of dust, and the soul "high." By thus valuing these two supposed-to-be parts, we inevitably throw them into competition with each other, like two corporations. The "spiritual" view, of course, has been that the body, in Yeats's phrase, must be "bruised to pleasure soul." And the "secular" version of the same dualism has been that the body, along with the rest of the "material" world, must give way before the advance of the human mind. The dominant religious view, for a long time, has been that the body is a kind of scrip issued by the Great Company Store in the Sky, which can be cashed in to redeem the soul but is otherwise worthless. And the predictable result has been a human creature able to appreciate or tolerate only the "spiritual" (or mental) part of Creation and full of semiconscious hatred of the "physical" or "natural" part, which it is ready and willing to destroy for "salvation," for profit, for "victory," or for fun. This madness constitutes the norm of modern humanity and of modern Christianity.

But to despise the body or mistreat it for the sake

of the "soul" is not just to burn one's house for the insurance, nor is it just self-hatred of the most deep and dangerous sort. It is yet another blasphemy. It is to make nothing—and worse than nothing—of the great Something in which we live and move and have our being.

When we hate and abuse the body and its earthly life and joy for Heaven's sake, what do we expect? That out of this life that we have presumed to despise and this world that we have presumed to destroy, we would somehow salvage a soul capable of eternal bliss? And what do we expect when with equal and opposite ingratitude, we try to make of the finite body an infinite reservoir of dispirited and meaningless pleasures?

Times may come, of course, when the life of the body must be denied or sacrificed, times when the whole world must literally be lost for the sake of one's life as a "living soul." But such sacrifice, by people who truly respect and revere the life of the earth and its Creator, does not denounce or degrade the body but rather exalts it and acknowledges its holiness. Such sacrifice is a refusal to allow the body to serve what is unworthy of it.

v

If we credit the Bible's description of the relationship between Creator and Creation, then we cannot deny the spiritual importance of our economic life. Then we must see how religious issues lead to issues of economy and how issues of economy lead to issues of art. By "art" I mean all the ways by which humans make the things they need. If we understand that no artist—no maker—can work except by reworking the works of Creation, then we see that by our work we reveal what we think of the works of God. How we take our lives from this world, how we work, what work we do, how well we use the materials we use, and what we do with them after we have used them—all these are questions of the highest and gravest religious significance. In answering them, we practice, or do not practice, our religion.

The significance—and ultimately the quality—of the work we do is determined by our understanding of the story in which we are taking part.

If we think of ourselves as merely biological creatures, whose story is determined by genetics or environment or history or economics or technology, then, however pleasant or painful the part we play, it cannot matter much. Its significance is that of mere self-concern. "It is a tale / Told by an idiot, full of sound and fury, / Signifying nothing," as Macbeth says when he has "supp'd full with horrors" and is "aweary of the sun."[18]

If we think of ourselves as lofty souls trapped temporarily in lowly bodies in a dispirited, desperate, unlovable world that we must despise for Heaven's sake, then what have we done for this question of significance? If we divide reality into two parts, spiritual and material, and hold (as the Bible does *not* hold) that only the spiritual is good or desirable, then our relation to the material Creation becomes arbitrary, having only the quantitative or mercenary value that we have, in fact and for this reason, assigned to it. Thus, we become the judges and inevitably the destroyers of a world we did not make and that we are bidden to understand as a divine gift. It is impossible to see how good work might be accomplished by people who think that our life in this world either signifies nothing or has only a negative significance.

If, on the other hand, we believe that we are living souls, God's dust and God's breath, acting our parts among other creatures all made of the same dust and breath as ourselves; and if we understand that we are free, within the obvious limits of mortal human life, to do evil or good to ourselves and to the other creatures —then all our acts have a supreme significance. If it is true that we are living souls and morally free, then all of us are artists. All of us are makers, within mortal terms and limits, of our lives, of one another's lives, of things we need and use.

This, Ananda Coomaraswamy wrote, is "the normal view," which "assumes . . . not that the artist is a special kind of man, but that every man who is not a mere idler or parasite is necessarily some special kind of artist."[19] But since even mere idlers and parasites may be said to work inescapably, by proxy or influence, it might be better to say that everybody is an artist— either good or bad, responsible or irresponsible. Any life, by working or not working, by working well or poorly, inescapably changes other lives and so changes the world. This is why our division of the "fine arts" from "craftsmanship," and "craftsmanship" from "labor," is so arbitrary, meaningless, and destructive. As Walter Shewring rightly said, both "the plowman and the potter have a cosmic function."[20] And bad art in any trade dishonors and damages Creation.

If we think of ourselves as living souls, immortal creatures, living in the midst of a Creation that is mostly mysterious, and if we see that everything we make or do cannot help but have an everlasting significance for ourselves, for others, and for the world, then we see why some religious teachers have understood work as a form of prayer. We see why the old poets invoked the muse. And we know why George Herbert prayed, in his poem "Mattens":

> Teach me thy love to know;
> That this new light, which now I see,
> May both the work and workman show.[21]

Work connects us both to Creation and to eternity. This is the reason also for Mother Ann Lee's famous instruction: "Do all your work as though you had a thousand years to live on earth, and as you would if you knew you must die tomorrow."[22]

Explaining "the perfection, order, and illumination" of the artistry of Shaker furniture makers, Coomaraswamy wrote, "All tradition has seen in the Master Craftsman of the Universe the exemplar of the human artist or 'maker by art,' and we are told to be 'perfect, *even as* your Father in heaven is perfect.' " Searching out the lesson, for us, of the Shakers' humble, impersonal, perfect artistry, which refused the modern divorce of utility and beauty, he wrote, "Unfortunately, we do not desire to be such as the Shaker was; we do not propose to 'work as though we had a thousand years to live, and as though we were to die tomorrow.' Just as we desire peace but not the things that make for peace, so we desire art but not the things that make for art. . . . we have the art that we deserve. If the sight of it puts us to shame, it is with ourselves that the reformation must begin."[23]

Any genuine effort to "re-form" our arts, our ways of making, must take thought of "the things that make for art." We must see that no art begins in itself; it begins in other arts, in attitudes and ideas antecedent to any art, in nature, and in inspiration. If we look at the great artistic traditions, as it is necessary to do, we will see that they have never been divorced either from religion or from economy. The possibility of an entirely secular art and of works of art that are spiritless or ugly or useless is not a possibility that has been among us for very long. Traditionally, the arts have been ways of making that have placed a just value on their materials or subjects, on the uses and the users of the things made by art, and on the artists themselves. They have, that is, been ways of giving honor to the works of God. The great artistic traditions have had nothing to do with what we call "self-expression." They have not been destructive of privacy or exploitive of private life. Though they have certainly originated things and employed genius, they have no affinity with the modern cults of originality and genius. Coomaraswamy, a good guide as always, makes an indispensable distinction between genius in the modern sense and craftsmanship: "Genius inhabits a world of its own. The master craftsman lives in a world inhabited by other men; he has neighbors."[24] The arts, traditionally, belong to the neighborhood. They are the means by which the neighborhood lives, works, remembers, worships, and enjoys itself.

But most important of all, now, is to see that the artistic traditions understood every art primarily as a skill or craft and ultimately as a service to fellow creatures and to God. An artist's first duty, according to this view, is technical. It is assumed that one will have talents, materials, subjects—perhaps even genius or inspiration or vision. But these are traditionally understood not as personal properties with which one may do as one chooses but as gifts of God or nature that must be honored in use. One does not dare to use these things without the skill to use them well. As Dante said of his own art, "far worse than in vain does he leave the shore . . . who fishes for the truth and has not the art."[25] To use gifts less than well is to dishonor them and their Giver. There is no material or subject in Creation that in using, we are excused from using well; there is no work in which we are excused from being able and responsible artists.

VI

In denying the holiness of the body and of the so-called physical reality of the world—and in denying support to the good economy, the good work, by which alone the Creation can receive due honor—modern Christianity generally has cut itself off from both nature and culture. It has no serious or competent interest in biology or ecology. And it is equally uninterested in the arts by which humankind connects itself to nature. It manifests no awareness of the specifically Christian cultural lineages that connect us to our past. There is, for example, a splendid heritage of Christian poetry in English that most church members live and die without reading or hearing or hearing about. Most sermons are preached without any awareness at all that the making of sermons is an art that has at times been magnificent. Most modern churches look like they were built by robots without reference to the heritage of church architecture or respect for the place; they embody no awareness that work can be worship. Most religious music now attests to the general assumption that religion is no more than a vaguely pious (and vaguely romantic) emotion.

Modern Christianity, then, has become as specialized in its organizations as other modern organizations, wholly concentrated on the industrial shibboleths of "growth," counting its success in numbers, and on the very strange enterprise of "saving" the individual, isolated, and disembodied soul. Having witnessed and abetted the dismemberment of the households, both human and natural, by which we have our being as creatures of God, as living souls, and having made light of the great feast and festival of Creation to which we were bidden as living souls, the modern church presumes to be able to save the soul as an eternal piece of private property. It presumes moreover to save the souls of people in other countries and religious traditions, who are often saner and more religious than we are. And always the emphasis is on the individual soul. Some Christian spokespeople give the impression that the highest Christian bliss would be to get to Heaven and find that you are the only one there—that you were right and all the others wrong. Whatever its twentieth-century dress, modern Christianity as I know it is still at bottom the religion of Miss Watson, intent on a dull and superstitious rigmarole by which supposedly we can avoid going to "the bad place" and instead go to "the good place." One can hardly help sympathizing with Huck Finn when he says, "I made up my mind I wouldn't try for it."[26]

Despite its protests to the contrary, modern Christianity has become willy-nilly the religion of the state and the economic status quo. Because it has been so exclusively dedicated to incanting anemic souls into Heaven, it has been made the tool of much earthly villainy. It has, for the most part, stood silently by while a predatory economy has ravaged the world, destroyed its natural beauty and health, divided and plundered its human communities and households. It has flown the flag and chanted the slogans of empire. It has assumed with the economists that "economic forces" automatically work for good and has assumed with the industrialists and militarists that technology determines history. It has assumed with almost everybody that "progress" is good, that it is good to be modern and up with the times. It has admired Caesar and comforted him in his depredations and defaults. But in its de facto alliance with Caesar, Christianity connives directly in the murder of Creation. For in these days, Caesar is no longer a mere destroyer of armies, cities, and nations. He is a contradicter of the fundamental miracle of life. A part of the normal practice of his power is his willingness to destroy the world. He prays, he says, and churches everywhere compliantly pray with him. But he is praying to a God whose works he is prepared at any moment to destroy. What could be more wicked than that, or more mad?

The religion of the Bible, on the contrary, is a religion of the state and the status quo only in brief moments. In practice, it is a religion for the correction equally of people and of kings. And Christ's life, from the manger to the cross, was an affront to the established powers of his time, just as it is to the established powers of our time. Much is made in churches of the "good news" of the Gospels. Less is said of the Gospels' bad news, which is that Jesus would have been horrified by just about every "Christian" government the world has ever seen. He would be horrified by our government and its works, and it would be horrified by him. Surely no sane and thoughtful person can imagine any government of our time sitting comfortably at the feet of Jesus while he is saying, "Love your enemies, bless them that curse you, do good to them that hate you, and pray for them that despitefully use you and persecute you."[27]

In fact, we know that one of the businesses of governments, "Christian" or not, has been to reenact the crucifixion. It has happened again and again and again. In *A Time for Trumpets*, his history of the Battle of the Bulge, Charles B. MacDonald tells how the SS Colonel Joachim Peiper was forced to withdraw from a bombarded château near the town of La Gleize, leaving behind a number of severely wounded soldiers of both armies. "Also left behind," MacDonald wrote, "on a whitewashed wall of one of the rooms in the basement was a charcoal drawing of Christ, thorns on his head, tears on his cheeks—whether drawn by a German or an American nobody would ever know."[28] This is not an image that belongs to history but rather one that judges it.

—1992

SEX, ECONOMY, FREEDOM, AND COMMUNITY

"It all turns on affection now," said Margaret. "Affection. Don't you see?"

—E. M. Forster, *Howards End*[1]

I

The sexual harassment phase of the Clarence Thomas hearing was handled by the news media as if it were anomalous and surprising. In fact, it was only an unusually spectacular revelation of the destructiveness of a process that has been well established and well respected for at least two hundred years—the process, that is, of community disintegration. This process has been well established and well respected for so long, of course, because it has been immensely profitable to those in a position to profit. The surprise and dismay occasioned by the Thomas hearing were not caused by the gossip involved (for that, the media had prepared us very well) but by the inescapable message that this process of disintegration, so little acknowledged by politicians and commentators, can be severely and perhaps illimitably destructive.

In the government-sponsored quarrel between Clarence Thomas and Anita Hill, public life collided with private life in a way that could not have been resolved and that could only have been damaging. The event was depressing and fearful both because of its violations of due process and justice and because it was an attempt to deal publicly with a problem for which there is no public solution. It embroiled the United States Senate in the impossible task of adjudicating alleged offenses that had occurred in private, of which there were no witnesses and no evidence. If the hearing was a "lynching," as Clarence Thomas said it was, that was because it dealt a public punishment to an unconvicted and unindicted victim. But it was a peculiar lynching, all the same, for it dealt the punishment equally to the accuser. It was not a hearing, much less a trial; it was a story-telling contest that was not winnable by either participant.

Its only result was damage to all participants and to the nation. Public life obviously cannot be conducted in that way, and neither can private life. It was a public procedure that degenerated into a private quarrel. It was a private quarrel that became a public catastrophe.

Sexual harassment, like most sexual conduct, is extremely dangerous as a public issue. A public issue, properly speaking, can only be an issue about which the public can confidently know. Because most sexual conduct is private, occurring only between two people, there are typically no witnesses. Apart from the possibility of a confession, the public can know about it only as a probably unjudgeable contest of stories. (In those rare instances when a sexual offense occurs before reliable witnesses, then, of course, it is a legitimate public issue.)

Does this mean that sexual conduct is *only* private in its interest and meaning? It certainly does not. For if there is no satisfactory way to deal publicly with sexual issues, there is also no satisfactory way to deal with them in mere privacy. To make sense of sexual issues or of sex itself, a third term, a third entity, has to intervene between public and private. For sex is not and cannot be any individual's "own business," nor is it merely the private concern of any couple. Sex, like any other necessary, precious, and volatile power that is commonly held, is everybody's business. A way must be found to entitle everybody's legitimate interest in it without either violating its essential privacy or allowing its unrestrained energies to reduce necessary public procedures to the level of a private quarrel. For sexual problems and potentialities that have a more-than-private interest, what is needed are common or shared forms and solutions that are not, in the usual sense, public.

The indispensable form that can intervene between public and private interests is that of community. The concerns of public and private, republic and citizen, necessary as they are, are not adequate for the shaping of human life. Community alone, as principle and as fact, can raise the standards of local health (ecological, economic, social, and spiritual) without which the other two interests will destroy one another.

By community, I mean the commonwealth and common interests, commonly understood, of people living together in a place and wishing to continue to do so. To put it another way, community is a locally understood interdependence of local people, local culture, local economy, and local nature. (Community, of course, is an idea that can extend itself beyond the local, but it only does so metaphorically. The idea of a national or global community is meaningless apart from the realization of local communities.) Lacking the interest of or in such a community, private life becomes merely a sort of reserve in which individuals defend their "right" to act as they please and attempt to limit or destroy the "rights" of other individuals to act as they please.

A community identifies itself by an understood mutuality of interests. But it lives and acts by the common virtues of trust, goodwill, forbearance, self-restraint, compassion, and forgiveness. If it hopes to continue long as a community, it will wish to—and will have to— encourage respect for all its members, human and natural. It will encourage respect for all stations and occupations. Such a community has the power—not invariably but as a rule—to enforce decency without litigation. It has the power, that is, to influence behavior. And it exercises this power not by coercion or violence but by teaching the young and by preserving stories and songs that tell (among other things) what works and what does not work in a given place.

Such a community is (among other things) a set of arrangements between men and women. These arrangements include marriage, family structure, divisions of work and authority, and responsibility for the instruction of children and young people. These arrangements exist, in part, to reduce the volatility and the danger of sex—to preserve its energy, its beauty, and its pleasure; to preserve and clarify its power to join not just husband

and wife to one another but parents to children, families to the community, the community to nature; to ensure, so far as possible, that the inheritors of sexuality, as they come of age, will be worthy of it.

But the life of a community is more vulnerable than public life. A community cannot be made or preserved apart from the loyalty and affection of its members and the respect and goodwill of the people outside it. And for a long time, these conditions have not been met. As the technological, economic, and political means of exploitation have expanded, communities have been more and more victimized by opportunists outside themselves. And as the salesmen, saleswomen, advertisers, and propagandists of the industrial economy have become more ubiquitous and more adept at seduction, communities have lost the loyalty and affection of their members. The community, wherever you look, is being destroyed by the desires and ambitions of both private and public life, which for want of the intervention of community interests are also destroying one another. Community life is by definition a life of cooperation and responsibility. Private life and public life, without the disciplines of community interest, necessarily gravitate toward competition and exploitation. As private life casts off all community restraints in the interest of economic exploitation or ambition or self-realization or whatever, the communal supports of public life also and by the same stroke are undercut, and public life becomes simply the arena of unrestrained private ambition and greed.

As our communities have disintegrated from external predation and internal disaffection, we have changed from a society whose ideal of justice was trust and fairness among people who knew each other into a society whose ideal of justice is public litigation, breeding distrust even among people who know each other.

Once it has shrugged off the interests and claims of the community, the public language of sexuality comes directly under the influence of private lust, ambition, and greed and becomes inadequate to deal with the real issues and problems of sexuality. The public dialogue degenerates into a stupefying and useless contest between so-called liberation and so-called morality. The real issues and problems, as they are experienced and suffered in people's lives, cannot be talked about. The public language can deal, however awkwardly and perhaps uselessly, with pornography, sexual hygiene, contraception, sexual harassment, rape, and so on. But it cannot talk about respect, responsibility, sexual discipline, fidelity, or the practice of love. "Sexual education," carried on in this public language, is and can only be a dispirited description of the working of a sort of anatomical machinery—and this is a sexuality that is neither erotic nor social nor sacramental but rather a cold-blooded, abstract procedure that is finally not even imaginable.

The conventional public opposition of "liberal" and "conservative" is, here as elsewhere, perfectly useless. The "conservatives" promote the family as a sort of public icon, but they will not promote the economic integrity of the household or the community, which are the mainstays of family life. Under the sponsorship of "conservative" presidencies, the economy of the modern household, which once required the father to work away from home—a development that was bad enough—now requires the mother to work away from home, as well. And this development has the wholehearted endorsement of "liberals," who see the mother thus forced to spend her days away from her home and children as "liberated"—though nobody has yet seen the fathers thus forced away as "liberated." Some feminists are thus in the curious position of opposing the mistreatment of women and yet advocating their participation in an economy in which everything is mistreated.

The "conservatives" more or less attack homosexuality, abortion, and pornography, and the "liberals" more or less defend them. Neither party will oppose sexual promiscuity. The "liberals" will not oppose promiscuity because they do not wish to appear intolerant of "individual liberty." The "conservatives" will not oppose promiscuity because sexual discipline would reduce the profits of corporations, which in their advertisements and entertainments encourage sexual self-indulgence as a way of selling merchandise.

The public discussion of sexual issues has thus degenerated into a poor attempt to equivocate between private lusts and public emergencies. Nowhere in public life (that is, in the public life that counts: the discussions of political and corporate leaders) is there an attempt to respond to community needs in the language of community interest.

And although we seem more and more inclined to look on education, even as it teaches less and is more overcome by violence, as the solution to all our problems (thus delaying the solution for a generation), there is really not much use in looking to education for the help we need. For education has become increasingly useless as it has become increasingly public. Real education is determined by community needs, not by public tests. Nor is community interest or community need going to receive much help from television and the other public media. Television is the greatest disrespecter and exploiter of sexuality that the world has ever seen; even if the network executives decide to promote "safe sex" and the use of condoms, they will not cease to pimp for the exceedingly profitable "sexual revolution." It is, in fact, the nature of the electronic media to blur and finally destroy all distinctions between public and community. Television has greatly accelerated the process, begun long ago, by which many communities have been atomized and congealed into one public. Nor is government a likely source of help. As political leaders have squirmed free of the claims and responsibilities of community life, public life has become their private preserve. The public political voice has become increasingly the voice of a conscious and self-serving duplicity: it is now, for instance, merely typical that a political leader can speak of "the preciousness of all life" while armed for the annihilation of all life. And the right of privacy, without the intervening claims and responsibilities of community life, has moved from the individual to the government and assumed the name of "official secrecy." Whose liberation is that?

In fact, there is no one to speak for the community interest except those people who wish to adhere to community principles. The community, in other words, must speak in its own interest. It must learn to defend itself. And in its self-defense, it may use the many powerful arguments provided for it by the failures of the private and public aims that have so nearly destroyed it.

The defenders of community should point out, for example, that for the joining of men and women there need to be many forms that only a community can provide. If you destroy the ideal of the "gentle man" and remove from men all expectations of courtesy and consideration toward women and children, you have prepared the way for an epidemic of rape and abuse. If you depreciate the sanctity and solemnity of marriage, not just as a bond between two people but as a bond between those two people and their forebears, their children, and their neighbors, then you have prepared the way for an epidemic of divorce, child neglect, community ruin, and loneliness. If you destroy the economies of household and community, then you destroy the bonds of mutual usefulness and practical dependence without which the other bonds will not hold.

If these and all other community-made arrangements between men and women are removed, if the only arrangements left between them are those of sex and sexual politics, instinct and polity without culture, then sex and politics are headed not only toward many kinds of private and public suffering but toward the destruction of justice, as in the confrontation of Clarence Thomas and Anita Hill.

II

But to deal with community disintegration as merely a matter of sexual disorder, however destructive that disorder may be, is misleading. The problem is far more complex than I have been able to suggest so far. There is much more to be said on the issue of sex, and I will return to it, but for the sake of both truth and clarity I must first examine other issues that are related and, in some respects, analogous to the issue of sex.

It is certain, as I have already said, that communities are destroyed both from within and from without: by internal disaffection and external exploitation. It is certain, too, that there have always been people who have become estranged from their communities for reasons of honest difference or disagreement. But it can be argued that community disintegration typically is begun by an aggression of some sort from the outside and that in modern times the typical aggression has been economic. The destruction of the community begins when its economy is made—not *dependent* (for no community has ever been entirely independent)—but *subject* to a larger external economy. As an example, we could probably do no better than the following account of the destruction of the local wool economy of the parish of Hawkshead in the Lake District of England:

> The . . . reason for the decline of the customary tenant must be sought in the introduction of machinery towards the end of the eighteenth century, which extinguished not only the local spinning and weaving, but was also the deathblow of the local market. Before this time, idleness at a fellside farm was unknown, for clothes and even linen were home-made, and all spare time was occupied by the youths in carding wool, while the girls spun the "garn" with distaff and wheel. . . . The sale of the yarn to the local weavers, and at the local market, brought important profits to the dalesman, so that it not only kept all hands busy, but put money into his pocket. But the introduction of machinery for looms and for spinning, and consequent outside demand for fleeces instead of yarn and woven material, threw idle not only half of the family, but the local hand-weavers, who were no doubt younger sons of the same stock. Thus idleness took the place of thrift and industry among a naturally industrious class, for the sons and daughters of the 'statesmen, often too proud to go out to service, became useless encumbrances on the estates. Then

came the improvement in agricultural methods [that is, technological innovations], which the 'statesman could not afford to keep abreast of. . . . What else could take place but that which did? The estates became mortgaged and were sold, and the rich manufacturers, whose villas are on the margin of Windermere, have often enough among their servants the actual descendants of the old 'statesmen, whose manufactures they first usurped and whose estates they afterwards absorbed.[2]

This paragraph sets forth the pattern of industrial exploitation of a locality and a local economy, a pattern that has prevailed for two hundred years. The industrialization of the eastern Kentucky coal fields early in the present century, though more violent, followed this pattern exactly.[3] A decentralized, fairly independent local economy was absorbed and destroyed by an aggressive, monetarily powerful outside economy. And like the displaced farmers, spinners, and weavers of Hawkshead, the once-independent mountaineers of eastern Kentucky became the wage-earning servants of those who had dispossessed their parents, sometimes digging the very coal that their families had once owned and had sold for as little per acre as the pittance the companies paid per day. By now, there is hardly a rural neighborhood or town in the United States that has not suffered some version of this process.

The same process is destroying local economies and cultures all over the world. Of Ladakh, for example, Helena Norberg-Hodge writes:

In the traditional culture, villagers provided for their basic needs without money. They had developed skills that enabled them to grow barley at 12,000 feet and to manage

> *yaks and other animals at even higher elevations. People knew how to build houses with their own hands from the materials of the immediate surroundings. The only thing they actually needed from outside the region was salt, for which they traded. They used money in only a limited way, mainly for luxuries.*
>
> *Now, suddenly, as part of the international money economy, Ladakhis find themselves ever more dependent— even for vital needs—on a system that is controlled by faraway forces. They are vulnerable to decisions made by people who do not even know that Ladakh exists. . . . For two thousand years in Ladakh, a kilo of barley has been a kilo of barley, but now you cannot be sure of its value.*[4]

This, I think, speaks for itself: if you are dependent on people who do not know you, who control the value of your necessities, you are not free, and you are not safe.

The industrial revolution has thus made universal the colonialist principle that has proved to be ruinous beyond measure: the assumption that it is permissible to ruin one place or culture for the sake of another. Thus justified or excused, the industrial economy grows in power and thrives on its damages to local economies, communities, and places. Meanwhile, politicians and bureaucrats measure the economic prosperity of their nations according to the burgeoning wealth of the industrial interests, not according to the success or failure of small local economies or the reduction and often hopeless servitude of local people. The self-congratulation of the industrialists and their political minions has continued unabated to this day. And yet it is a fact that the industrialists of Hawkshead, like all those elsewhere and since, have lived off the public, just as surely as do the despised clients of "welfare." They have lived off a

public of industrially destroyed communities, and they
have not compensated for this destruction by their os-
tentatious contributions to the art, culture, and education of the professional class, or by their "charities"
to the poor. Nor is this state of things ameliorated by
efforts to enable a local population to "participate" in
the global economy, by "education" or any other means.
It is true that local individuals, depending on their capital, intelligence, cunning, or influence, may be able to
"participate" to their apparent advantage, but local communities and places can "participate" only as victims.
The global economy does not exist to help the communities and localities of the globe. It exists to siphon
the wealth of those communities and places into a few
bank accounts. To this economy, democracy and the
values of the religious traditions mean absolutely nothing. And those who wish to help communities to
survive had better understand that a merely political
freedom means little within a totalitarian economy.
Ms. Norberg-Hodge says, of the relatively new influence of the global economy on Ladakh, that

> *Increasingly, people are locked into an economic system*
> *that pumps resources out of the periphery into the center*
> *—from the nonindustrialized to the industrialized parts*
> *of the world, from the countryside to the city, from the*
> *poor to the rich. Often, these resources end up back where*
> *they came from as commercial products . . . at prices that*
> *the poor can no longer afford.*[5]

This is an apt description not just of what is happening
in Ladakh but of what is happening in my own rural
county and in every other rural county in the United
States.

The situation in the wool economy of Hawkshead at the end of the eighteenth century was the same as that which, a little later, caused the brief uprising of those workers in England who were called Luddites. These were people who dared to assert that there were needs and values that justly took precedence over industrialization; they were people who rejected the determinism of technological innovation and economic exploitation. In them, the community attempted to speak for itself and defend itself. It happened that Lord Byron's maiden speech in the House of Lords, on February 27, 1812, dealt with the uprising of the Luddites, and this, in part, is what he said:

> By the adoption of one species of [weaving] frame in particular, one man performed the work of many, and the superfluous laborers were thrown out of employment. Yet it is to be observed, that the work thus executed was inferior in quality; not marketable at home, and merely hurried over with a view to exportation. . . . The rejected workmen . . . conceived themselves to be sacrificed to improvements in mechanism. In the foolishness of their hearts they imagined that the maintenance and well-doing of the industrious poor were objects of greater importance than the enrichment of a few individuals by any improvement, in the implements of trade, which threw the workmen out of employment, and rendered the laborer unworthy of his hire.[6]

The Luddites did, in fact, revolt not only against their own economic oppression but also against the poor quality of the machine work that had replaced them. And though they destroyed machinery, they "abstained from bloodshed or violence against living beings, until in 1812 a band of them was shot down by soldiers." Their movement was suppressed by "severe repressive legislation" and by "many hangings and transportations."[7]

The Luddites thus asserted the precedence of community needs over technological innovation and monetary profit, and they were dealt with in a way that seems merely inevitable in the light of subsequent history. In the years since, the only group that I know of that has successfully, so far, made the community the standard of technological innovation has been the Amish. The Amish have differed from the Luddites in that they have not destroyed but merely declined to use the technologies that they perceive as threatening to their community. And this has been possible because the Amish are an agrarian people. The Luddites could not have refused the machinery that they destroyed; the machinery had refused them.

The victory of industrialism over Luddism was thus overwhelming and unconditional; it was undoubtedly the most complete, significant, and lasting victory of modern times. And so one must wonder at the intensity with which any suggestion of Luddism still is feared and hated. To this day, if you say you would be willing to forbid, restrict, or reduce the use of technological devices in order to protect the community—or to protect the good health of nature on which the community depends—you will be called a Luddite, and it will not be a compliment. To say that the community is more important than machines is certainly Christian and certainly democratic, but it is also Luddism and therefore not to be tolerated.

Technological determinism, then, has triumphed. By now the rhetoric of technological determinism has become thoroughly mixed with the rhetoric of national mysticism so that a political leader may confidently say that it is "our destiny" to go to the moon or Mars or wherever we may go for the profit of those who will provide the transportation. Because this "destiny" has become the all-shaping superstition of our time and is therefore never debated in public, we have difficulty seeing that the triumph of technological determinism is the defeat of community. But it is a fact that in both private conversation and public dialogue, the community has neither status nor standing from which to plead in its own defense. There is no denying, of course, that "community" ranks with "family," "our land," and "our beloved country" as an icon of the public vocabulary; everybody is for it, and this means nothing. If individuals or groups have the temerity to oppose an actual item on the agenda of technological process because it will damage a community, the powers that be will think them guilty of Luddism, sedition, and perhaps insanity. Local and community organizations, of course, do at times prevail over the would-be "developers," but the status of these victories remains tentative. The powers that be, and the media as well, treat such victories as anomalies, never as the work of a legitimate "side" in the public dialogue.

Some time ago, for example, my friends in the Community Farm Alliance asked me to write a newspaper piece opposing the Bush administration's efforts to revise the General Agreement on Tariffs and Trade; the proposed revisions would destroy all barriers and restrictions to international trade in food, thus threatening the already precarious survival of farm communities in the industrial countries and also the local availability of food in Third World countries. I wrote the article and sent it to the editor of the op-ed page of the *New York*

Times, who had invited me to make such submissions —and who rejected my article on the ground that the subject was "not sexy." I conclude that if the opponents of the GATT revisions should win, their victory will have an effect limited to the issue—that is, such a victory would not cause their point of view to be acknowledged, much less represented, among the powers that be, and the public standing of community interests would be no higher than before.

The triumph of the industrial economy is the fall of community. But the fall of community reveals how precious and how necessary community is. For when community falls, so must fall all the things that only community life can engender and protect: the care of the old, the care and education of children, family life, neighborly work, the handing down of memory, the care of the earth, respect for nature and the lives of wild creatures. All of these things have been damaged by the rule of industrialism, but of all the damaged things probably the most precious and the most damaged is sexual love. For sexual love is the heart of community life. Sexual love is the force that in our bodily life connects us most intimately to the Creation, to the fertility of the world, to farming and the care of animals. It brings us into the dance that holds the community together and joins it to its place.

In dealing with community, as in dealing with everything else, the industrial economy goes for the nucleus. It does this because it wants the power to cause fundamental change. To make sex the preferred bait of commerce may seem merely the obvious thing to do, once greed is granted its now conventional priority as a motive. But this could happen only after a probably instinctive sense of the sanctity and dignity of the body—the sense of its having been "fearfully and wonderfully made"[8]—had been destroyed. Once this ancient reticence had been broken down, then the come-on of the pimp could be instituted as the universal spiel of the marketplace; everything could be sold on the promise of instant, innocent sexual gratification, "no strings attached." Sexual energy cannot be made publicly available for commercial use—that is, prostituted —without destroying all of its communal or cultural forms: forms of courtship, marriage, family life, household economy, and so on. The devaluation of sexuality, like the devaluation of a monetary currency, destroys its correspondence to other values.

In the wake of the Thomas-Hill catastrophe in Washington, the *New York Times Sunday Magazine* contained a skin lotion advertisement that displayed a photograph of the naked torso of a woman. From a feminist point of view, this headless and footless body represents the male chauvinist's sexual ideal: a woman who cannot think and cannot escape. From a point of view somewhat more comprehensive—the point of view of community—it represents also the commercial ideal of the industrial economy: the completely seducible consumer, unable either to judge or to resist.

The headlessness of this lotionable lady suggests also another telling indication of the devaluation of sexual love in modern times—that is, the gravitation of attention from the countenance, especially the eyes, to the specifically sexual anatomy. The difference, of course, is that the countenance is both physical and spiritual. There is much testimony to this in the poetic tradition and elsewhere. Looking into one another's eyes, lovers recognize their encounter as a meeting not merely of two bodies but of two living souls. In one

another's eyes, moreover, they see themselves reflected
not narcissistically but as singular beings, separate and
small, far inferior to the creature that they together
make.

In this meeting of eyes, there is an acknowledgment
that love is more than sex:

> *'This Ecstasy doth unperplex,'*
> *We said, 'and tell us what we love;*
> *We see by this it was not sex;*
> *We see we saw not what did move.'*[9]

These lines are from John Donne's poem "The Ecstasy,"
in which the lovers have been joined by the "double
string" of their mutual gaze. This is not a disembodied
love. Far from it. For love is finally seen in the poem
as "that subtle knot, which makes us man" by joining
body and soul together, just as it joins the two lovers.
Sexual love is thus understood as both fact and mystery,
physical motion and spiritual motive. That this complex
love should be reduced simply to sex has always seemed
a fearful thing to the poets. As late as our own century,
for example, we have these lines from Wallace Stevens:

> *If sex were all, then every trembling hand*
> *Could make us squeak, like dolls, the wished-for words.*[10]

The fear of the reduction of love to sex is obviously
subject to distortion. At worst, this fear has caused a
kind of joyless prudery. But at best, it has been a just
fear, implying both an appropriate awe and a reluctance
that humans should become the puppets of a single
instinct. Such a puppetry is possible, and its sign, in
modern terms, is the body as product, made delectably

consumable by the application of lotions and other commercial liquids. But there is a higher, juster love of which the sign is the meeting of the eyes.

In the poetry that I know, the most graceful and the richest testimony to the power of the eyes is in act three, scene two, of *The Merchant of Venice*, where Portia says to Bassanio:

> *Beshrew your eyes,*
> *They have o'erlook'd me and divided me,*
> *One half of me is yours, the other half yours,—*
> *Mine own I would say: but if mine then yours,*
> *And so all yours.*

Portia is no headless woman. She is the brightest, most articulate character in the play. Witty and charming as these lines are, they are not frivolous. They attest to the sexual and the spiritual power of a look, which has just begun an endless conversation between two living souls. This speech of hers is as powerful as it is because she knows exactly what she is doing. What she is doing is giving herself away. She has entered into a situation in which she must find her life by losing it. She is glad, and she is frightened. She is speaking joyfully and fearfully of the self's suddenly irresistible wish to be given away. And this is an unconditional giving, on which, she knows, time and mortality will impose their inescapable conditions; she will have remembered the marriage ceremony with its warnings of difficulty, poverty, sickness, and death. There is nothing "safe" about this. This love has no place to happen except in this world, where it cannot be made safe. And this scene finally becomes a sort of wedding, in which Portia says to Bassanio, "Myself, and what is mine, to you and yours /

Is now converted. . . . I give them with this ring."

There is no "sexism" or "double standard" in this exchange of looks and what it leads to. The look of which Portia speaks could have had such power only because it answered a look of hers; she has, in the same moment, "o'erlook'd" Bassanio. She is not speaking as a woman submitting to the power of a man, much less to seduction. She is speaking as one of a pair who are submitting to the redemptive power of love. Responding to Portia's pledge of herself to him, Bassanio cannot say much; he is not so eloquent as she, and his mind has become "a wild of nothing, save of joy." He says only:

> *when this ring*
> *Parts from this finger, then parts life from hence,—*
> *O then be bold to say Bassanio's dead!*

But that is enough. He is saying, as his actual wedding will require him to say, that he will be true to Portia until death. But he is also saying, as she has said, that he is dead to his old life and can now live only in the new life of their love. He might have said, with Dante, "Of a surety I have now set my feet on that point of life, beyond the which he must not pass who would return."[11]

This is a play about the precedence of affection and fidelity over profit, and so it is a play about the order of community. Lovers must not, like usurers, live for themselves alone. They must finally turn from their gaze at one another back toward the community. If they had only themselves to consider, lovers would not need to marry, but they must think of others and of other things. They say their vows to the community as much as to one another, and the community gathers around them to hear and to wish them well, on their behalf and on its own. It gathers around them because it understands how necessary, how joyful, and how fearful this joining is. These lovers, pledging themselves to one another "until death," are giving themselves away, and they are joined by this as no law or contract could ever join them. Lovers, then, "die" into their union with one another as a soul "dies" into its union with God. And so here, at the very heart of community life, we find not something to sell as in the public market but this momentous giving. If the community cannot protect this giving, it can protect nothing—and our time is proving that this is so.

We thus can see that there are two kinds of human economy. There is the kind of economy that exists to protect the "right" of profit, as does our present public economy; this sort of economy will inevitably gravitate toward protection of the "rights" of those who profit most. Our present public economy is really a political system that safeguards the private exploitation of the public wealth and health. The other kind of economy exists for the protection of gifts, beginning with the "giving in marriage," and this is the economy of community, which now has been nearly destroyed by the public economy.

There are two kinds of sexuality that correspond to the two kinds of economy. The sexuality of community life, whatever its inevitable vagaries, is centered on marriage, which joins two living souls as closely as, in this world, they can be joined. This joining of two who know, love, and trust one another brings them in the same breath into the freedom of sexual consent and into the fullest earthly realization of the image of God. From their joining, other living souls come into being, and with them great responsibilities that are unending, fearful, and joyful. The marriage of two lovers joins them to one another, to forebears, to descendants, to the community, to Heaven and earth. It is the fundamental connection without which nothing holds, and trust is its necessity.

Our present sexual conduct, on the other hand, having "liberated" itself from the several trusts of community life, is public, like our present economy. It has forsaken trust, for it rests on the easy giving and breaking of promises. And having forsaken trust, it has predictably become political. In private life, as in public, we are attempting to correct bad character and low motives by law and by litigation. "Losing kindness," as Lao-tzu said, "they turn to justness."[12] The superstition of the anger of our current sexual politics, as of other kinds of anger, is that somewhere along the trajectory of any quarrel a tribunal will be reached that will hear all complaints and find for the plaintiff; the verdict will be that the defendant is entirely wrong, the plaintiff entirely right and entirely righteous. This, of course, is not going to happen. And because such "justice" cannot happen, litigation only prolongs itself. The difficulty is that marriage, family life, friendship, neighborhood, and other personal connections do not depend exclusively or even primarily on justice—though, of course, they all must try for it. They depend also on trust, patience, respect, mutual help, forgiveness—in other words, the *practice* of love, as opposed to the mere *feeling* of love.

As soon as the parties to a marriage or a friendship begin to require strict justice of each other, then that marriage or friendship begins to be destroyed, for there is no way to adjudicate the competing claims of a personal quarrel. And so these relationships do not dissolve into litigation, really; they dissolve into a feud, an endless exchange of accusations and retributions. If the two parties have not the grace to forgive the inevitable offenses of close connection, the next best thing is separation and silence. But why should separation have come to be the virtually conventional outcome of close relationships in our society? The proper question, perhaps, is not why we have so much divorce, but why we are so unforgiving. The answer, perhaps, is that, though we still recognize the feeling of love, we have forgotten how to practice love when we don't feel it.

Because of our determination to separate sex from the practice of love in marriage and in family and community life, our public sexual morality is confused, sentimental, bitter, complexly destructive, and hypocritical. It begins with the idea of "sexual liberation": whatever people desire is "natural" and all right, men and women are not different but merely equal, and all desires are equal. If a man wants to sit down while a pregnant woman is standing or walk through a heavy door and let it slam in a woman's face, that is all right. Divorce on an epidemic scale is all right; child abandonment by one parent or another is all right; it is regrettable but still pretty much all right if a divorced parent neglects or refuses to pay child support; promiscuity is all right; adultery is all right. Promiscuity among teenagers is pretty much all right, for "that's the way it is"; abortion as birth control is all right; the prostitution of sex in advertisements and public entertainment is all right. But then, far down this road of freedom, we decide that a few lines ought to be drawn. Child molestation, we wish to say, is not all right, nor is sexual violence, nor is sexual harassment, nor is pregnancy among unmarried teenagers. We are also against venereal diseases, the diseases of promiscuity, though we tend to think that they are the government's responsibility, not ours.

In this cult of liberated sexuality, "free" of courtesy, ceremony, responsibility, and restraint, dependent on litigation and expert advice, there is much that is human, sad to say, but there is no sense or sanity. Trying to draw the line where we are trying to draw it, between carelessness and brutality, is like insisting that falling is flying—until you hit the ground—and then trying to outlaw hitting the ground. The pretentious, fantastical, and solemn idiocy of the public sexual code could not be better exemplified than by the now-ubiquitous phrase "sexual partner," which denies all that is implied by the names of "husband" or "wife" or even "lover." It denies anyone's responsibility for the consequences of sex. With one's "sexual partner," it is now understood, one must practice "safe sex"—that is, one must protect oneself, not one's partner or the children that may come of the "partnership."

But the worst hypocrisy of all is in the failure of the sexual libertarians to come to the defense of sexually liberated politicians. The public applies strenuously to public officials a sexual morality that it no longer applies to anyone privately and that it does not apply to other liberated public figures, such as movie stars, artists, athletes, and business tycoons. The prurient squeamishness with which the public and the public media poke into the lives of politicians is surely not an expectable result of liberation. But this paradox is not the only one. According to its claims, sexual liberation ought logically to have brought in a time of "naturalness," ease, and candor between men and women. It has, on the contrary, filled the country with sexual self-consciousness, uncertainty, and fear. Women, though they may dress as if the sexual millennium had arrived, hurry along our city streets and public corridors with their eyes averted, like hunted animals. "Eye contact," once the very signature of our humanity, has become a danger. The meeting ground between men and women, which ought to be safeguarded by trust, has become a place of suspicion, competition, and violence. One no longer goes there asking how instinct may be ramified in affection and loyalty; now one asks how instinct may be indulged with the least risk to personal safety.

Seeking to "free" sexual love from its old communal restraints, we have "freed" it also from its meaning, its responsibility, and its exaltation. And we have made it more dangerous. "Sexual liberation" is as much a fraud and as great a failure as the "peaceful atom." We are now living in a sexual atmosphere so polluted and embittered that women must look on virtually any man as a potential assailant, and a man must look on virtually any woman as a potential accuser. The idea that this situation can be corrected by the courts and the police only compounds the disorder and the danger. And in the midst of this acid rainfall of predation and recrimination, we presume to teach our young people that sex can be made "safe"—by the use, inevitably, of purchased drugs and devices. What a lie! Sex was never safe, and it is less safe now than it has ever been.

What we are actually teaching the young is an illusion of thoughtless freedom and purchasable safety, which encourages them to tamper prematurely, disrespectfully, and dangerously with a great power. Just as the public economy encourages people to spend money and waste the world, so the public sexual code encourages people to be spendthrifts and squanderers of sex. The basis of true community and household economy, on the other hand, is thrift. The basis of community sexuality is respect for everything that is involved—and respect, here as everywhere, implies discipline. By their common principles of extravagance and undisciplined freedom, our public economy and our public sexuality are exploiting and spending moral capital built up by centuries of community life—exactly as industrial agriculture has been exploiting and spending the natural capital built up over thousands of years in the soil.

In sex, as in other things, we have liberated fantasy but killed imagination, and so have sealed ourselves in selfishness and loneliness. Fantasy is of the solitary self, and it cannot lead us away from ourselves. It is by imagination that we cross over the differences between ourselves and other beings and thus learn compassion, forbearance, mercy, forgiveness, sympathy, and love—the virtues without which neither we nor the world can live.

Starting with economic brutality, we have arrived at sexual brutality. Those who affirm the one and deplore the other will have to explain how we might logically have arrived anywhere else. Sexual lovemaking between humans is not and cannot be the thoughtless, instinctual coupling of animals; it is not "recreation"; it is not "safe." It is the strongest prompting and the greatest joy that young people are likely to experience. Because it is so powerful, it is risky, not just because of the famous dangers of venereal disease and "unwanted pregnancy" but also because it involves and requires a giving away of the self that if not honored and reciprocated, inevitably reduces dignity and self-respect.

The invitation to give oneself away is not, except for the extremely ignorant or the extremely foolish, an easy one to accept.

Perhaps the current revulsion against sexual harassment may be the beginning of a renewal of sexual responsibility and self-respect. It must, at any rate, be the beginning of a repudiation of the idea that sex among us is merely natural. If men and women are merely animals, it is hard to see how sexual harassment could have become an issue, for such harassment is no more than the instinctive procedure of male animals, who openly harass females, usually by unabashed physical display and contact; it is their way of asking who is and who is not in estrus. Women would not think such behavior offensive if we had not, for thousands of years, understood ourselves as specifically human beings—creatures who, if in some ways animal-like, are in other ways God-like. In asking men to feel shame and to restrain themselves—which one would not ask of an animal—women are implicitly asking to be treated as human beings in that full sense, as living souls made in the image of God. But any humans who wish to be treated and to treat others according to that definition must understand that this is not a kindness that can be conferred by a public economy or by a public government or by a public people. It can only be conferred on its members by a community.

III

Much of the modern assault on community life has been conducted within the justification and protection of the idea of freedom. Thus, it is necessary to try to see how the themes of freedom and community have intersected.

The idea of freedom, as Americans understand it, owes its existence to the inevitability that people will disagree. It is a way of guaranteeing to individuals and to political bodies the right to be different from one another. A specifically American freedom began with our wish to assert our differences from England, and its principles were then worked out in the effort to deal with differences among the states. The result is the Bill of Rights, of which the cornerstone is the freedom of speech. This freedom is not only the basic guarantee of political liberty but it also obligates public officials and private citizens alike to acknowledge the inherent dignity and worth of individual people. It exists only as an absolute; if it can be infringed at all, then probably it can be destroyed entirely.

But if it is an absolute, it is a peculiar and troubling one. It is not an absolute in the sense that a law of nature is. It is not absolute even as the moral law is. One person alone can uphold the moral law, but one person alone cannot uphold the freedom of speech. The freedom of speech is a public absolute, and it can remain absolute only so long as a sufficient segment of the public believes that it is and consents to uphold it. It is an absolute that can be destroyed by public opinion. This is where the danger lies. If this freedom is abused and if a sufficient segment of the public becomes sufficiently resentful of the abuses, then the freedom will be revoked. It is a freedom, therefore, that depends directly on responsibility. And so the First Amendment alone is not a sufficient guarantee of the freedom of speech.

As we now speak of it, freedom is almost always understood as a public idea having to do with the liberties of individuals. The public dialogue about freedom almost always has to do with the efforts of one group or another to wrest these individual liberties from the government or to protect them from another group. In this situation, it is inevitable that freedom will be understood as an issue of power. This is perhaps as necessary as it is unavoidable. But power is not the only issue related to freedom.

From another point of view, not necessarily incompatible, freedom has long been understood as the consequence of knowing the truth. When Jesus said to his followers, "Ye shall know the truth, and the truth shall make you free,"[13] he was not talking primarily about politics, but the political applicability of the statement has been obvious for a long time, especially to advocates of democracy. According to this line of thought, freedom of speech is necessary to political health and sanity because it permits speech—the public dialogue—to correct itself. Thomas Jefferson had this in mind when he said in his first inaugural address, "If there be any among us who would wish to dissolve this Union or to change its republican form, let them stand undisturbed as monuments of the safety with which error of opinion may be tolerated where reason is left free to combat it."[14] The often-cited "freedom to be wrong" is thus a valid freedom, but it is a poor thing by itself; its validity comes from the recognition that error is real, identifiable as such, dangerous to freedom as to much else, and controvertible. The freedom to be wrong is valid, in other words, because it is the unexcisable other half of the freedom to be right. If freedom is understood as merely the privilege of the unconcerned and uncommitted to muddle about in error, then freedom will certainly destroy itself.

But to define freedom only as a public privilege of private citizens is finally inadequate to the job of protecting freedom. It leaves the issue too public and too private. It fails to provide a circumstance for those private satisfactions and responsibilities without which freedom is both pointless and fragile. Here as elsewhere, we need to interpose between the public and the private interests a third interest: that of the community. When there is no forcible assertion of the interest of community, public freedom becomes a sort of refuge for escapees from the moral law—those who hold that there is, in Mary McGrory's words, "no ethical transgression except an indictable one."[15]

Public laws are meant for a public, and they vary, sometimes radically, according to forms of government. The moral law, which is remarkably consistent from one culture to another, has to do with community life. It tells us how we should treat relatives and neighbors and, by metaphorical extension, strangers. The aim of the moral law is the integrity and longevity of the community, just as the aim of public law is the integrity and longevity of a political body. Sometimes, the identities of community and political body are nearly the same, and in that case public laws are not necessary because there is, strictly speaking, no "public." As I understand the term, *public* means simply all the people, apart from any personal responsibility or belonging. A public building, for example, is a building which everyone may use but to which no one belongs, which belongs to everyone but not to anyone in particular, and for which no one is responsible except "public employees." A community, unlike a public, has to do first of all with belonging; it is a group of people who belong to one another and to their place. We would say, "We belong to our community," but never "We belong to our public."

I don't know when the concept of "the public," in our sense, emerged from the concept of "the people." But I am aware that there have been human situations in which the concept of "the public" was simply unnecessary. It is not quite possible, for example, to think of the Bushmen or the Eskimos as "publics" or of any parts of their homelands as "public places." And in the traditional rural villages of England there was no public place but rather a "common." A public, I suppose, becomes necessary when a political body grows so large as to include several divergent communities.

A public government, with public laws and a public system of justice, founded on democratic suffrage, is in principle a good thing. Ideally, it makes possible a just and peaceable settlement of contentions arising between communities. It also makes it possible for a mistreated member of a community to appeal for justice outside the community. But obviously such a government can fall short of its purpose. When a public government becomes identified with a public economy, a public culture, and public fashions of thought, it can become the tool of a public process of nationalism or "globalization" that is oblivious of local differences and therefore destructive of communities.

"Public" and "community," then, are different—perhaps radically different—concepts that under certain circumstances are compatible but that, in the present economic and technological monoculture, tend to be at odds. A community, when it is alive and well, is centered on the household—the family place and economy—and the household is centered on marriage.

A public, when it is working in the best way—that is, as a political body intent on justice—is centered on the individual. Community and public alike, then, are founded on respect—the one on respect for the family, the other on respect for the individual. Both forms of respect are deeply traditional, and they are not fundamentally incompatible. But they are different, and that difference, once it is instituted in general assumptions, can be the source of much damage and much danger.

A household, according to its nature, will seek to protect and prolong its own life, and since it will readily perceive its inability to survive alone, it will seek to join its life to the life of a community. A young person, coming of age in a healthy household and community, will understand her or his life in terms of membership and service. But in a public increasingly disaffected and turned away from community, it is clear that individuals must be increasingly disinclined to identify themselves in such a way.

The individual, unlike the household and the community, always has two ways to turn: she or he may turn either toward the household and the community, to receive membership and to give service, or toward the relatively unconditional life of the public, in which one is free to pursue self-realization, self-aggrandizement, self-interest, self-fulfillment, self-enrichment, self-promotion, and so on. The problem is that—unlike a married couple, a household, or a community—one individual represents no fecundity, no continuity, and no harmony. The individual life implies no standard of behavior or responsibility.

I am indebted to Judith Weissman for the perception that there are two kinds of freedom: the freedom of the community and the freedom of the individual.[16]

The freedom of the community is the more fundamental and the more complex. A community confers on its members the freedoms implicit in familiarity, mutual respect, mutual affection, and mutual help; it gives freedom its proper aims; and it prescribes or shows the responsibilities without which no one can be legitimately free, or free for very long. But to confer freedom or any other benefits on its members, a community must also be free from outside pressure or coercion. It must, in other words, be so far as possible the cause of its own changes; it must change in response to its own changing needs and local circumstances, not in response to motives, powers, or fashions coming from elsewhere. The freedom of the individual, by contrast, has been construed customarily as a license to pursue any legal self-interest at large and at will in the domain of public liberties and opportunities.

These two kinds of freedom, so understood, are clearly at odds. In modern times, the dominant freedom has been that of the individual, and Judith Weissman believes—correctly, I think—that this self-centered freedom is still the aim of contemporary liberation movements:

> *The liberation of the individual self for fulfillments, discoveries, pleasures, and joys, and the definition of oppression as mental and emotional constraints . . . this combination existing at the heart of Shelley's Romantic radicalism remains basically unchanged in later feminist writers. . . .* [17]

Freedom defined strictly as individual freedom tends to see itself as an escape from the constraints of community life—constraints necessarily implied by consideration for the nature of a place; by consideration for the needs and feelings of neighbors; by kindness to strangers; by respect for the privacy, dignity, and propriety of individual lives; by affection for a place, its people, and its nonhuman creatures; and by the duty to teach the young.

But certain liberationist intellectuals are not the only ones who have demanded this sort of freedom. Almost everybody now demands it, as she or he has been taught to do by the schools, by the various forms of public entertainment, and by salespeople, advertisers, and other public representatives of the industrial economy. People are instructed to free themselves of all restrictions, restraints, and scruples in order to fulfill themselves as individuals to the utmost extent that the law allows. Moreover, we treat corporations as "persons"—an abuse of a metaphor if ever there was one! —and allow to them the same liberation from community obligations that we allow to individuals.

But there is a paradox in all this, and it is as cruel as it is obvious: as the emphasis on individual liberty has increased, the liberty and power of most individuals has declined. Most people are now finding that they are free to make very few significant choices. It is becoming steadily harder for ordinary people—the unrich, the unprivileged—to choose a kind of work for which they have a preference, a talent, or a vocation, to choose where they will live, to choose to work (or to live) at home, or even to choose to raise their own children. And most individuals ("liberated" or not) choose to conform not to local ways and conditions but to a rootless and placeless monoculture of commercial expectations and products. We try to be "emotionally self-sufficient" at the same time that we are entirely and helplessly dependent for our "happiness" on an economy that abuses us along with everything else. We want the liberty of divorce from spouses and independence from family and friends, yet we remain indissolubly married to a hundred corporations that regard us at best as captives and at worst as prey. The net result of our much-asserted individualism appears to be that we have become "free" for the sake of not much self-fulfillment at all.

However frustrated, disappointed, and unfulfilled it may be, the pursuit of self-liberation is still the strongest force now operating in our society. It is the dominant purpose not only of those feminists whose individualism troubles Judith Weissman but also of virtually the entire population; it determines the ethics of the professional class; it defines increasingly the ambitions of politicians and other public servants. This purpose is publicly sanctioned and publicly supported, and it operates invariably to the detriment of community life and community values.

All the institutions that "serve the community" are publicly oriented: the schools, governments and government agencies, the professions, the corporations. Even the churches, though they may have community memberships, do not concern themselves with issues of local economy and local ecology on which community health and integrity must depend. Nor do the people in charge of these institutions think of themselves as members of communities. They are itinerant, in fact or in spirit, as their careers require them to be. These various public servants all have tended to impose on the local place and the local people programs, purposes, procedures, technologies, and values that originated elsewhere. Typically, these "services" involve a condescension to and a contempt for local life that are implicit in all the assumptions—woven into the very fabric—of the industrial economy.

A community, especially if it is a rural community, is understood by its public servants as provincial, backward and benighted, unmodern, unprogressive, unlike "us," and therefore in need of whatever changes are proposed for it by outside interests (to the profit of the outside interests). Anyone who thinks of herself or himself as a member of such a community will sooner or later see that the community is under attack morally as well as economically. And this attack masquerades invariably as altruism: the community must be plundered, expropriated, or morally offended for its own good—but its good is invariably defined by the interest of the invader. The community is not asked whether or not it wishes to be changed, or how it wishes to be changed, or what it wishes to be changed into. The community is deemed to be backward and provincial, it is taught to believe and to regret that it is backward and provincial, and it is thereby taught to welcome the purposes of its invaders.

I have already discussed at some length the honored practice of community destruction by economic invasion. Now it will be useful to look at an example of the analogous practice of moral invasion. In 1989, Actors Theater of Louisville presented the premiere performance of Arthur Kopit's play *Bone-the-Fish*. The Louisville *Courier-Journal* welcomed Mr. Kopit and his play to town with the headline: "Arthur Kopit plans to offend almost everyone." In the accompanying article, Mr. Kopit is quoted as saying of his play:

I am immodestly proud that it is written in consistently bad taste. It's about vile people who do vile things. They are totally loathsome, and I love them all. . . . I'm almost positive that it has something to offend everyone.

The writer of the article explains that "Kopit wrote 'Bone-the-Fish' out of a counterculture impulse, as a reaction against a complacency that he finds is corrupting American life."[18]

My interest here is not in the quality or the point of Mr. Kopit's play, which I did not see (because I do not willingly subject myself to offense). I am interested in the article about him and his play merely as an example of the conventionality of the artistic intention to offend—and of the complacency of the public willingness not to be offended but passively to accept offense. Here we see the famous playwright coming from the center of culture to a provincial city, declaring his intention to "offend almost everyone," and here we see the local drama critic deferentially explaining the moral purpose of this intention. But the playwright makes three rather curious assumptions: (1) that the Louisville theater audience may be supposed (without proof) to be complacent and corrupt; (2) that they therefore deserve to be offended; and (3) that being offended will make them less complacent and less corrupt.

That Louisville theatergoers are more complacent and corrupt than theatergoers elsewhere (or than Mr. Kopit) is not an issue, for there is no evidence. That they deserve to be offended is not an issue for the same reason. That anyone's complacency and corruption can be corrected by being offended in a theater is merely a contradiction in terms, for people who are corrupted by complacency are by definition not likely to take offense.

People who do take offense will be either fundamentally decent or aggressively corrupt. People who are fundamentally decent do not deserve to be offended and cannot be instructed by offense. People who are aggressively corrupt would perhaps see the offense but would not accept it. Mr. Kopit's preferred audience is therefore one that will applaud his audacity and pay no attention at all to his avowed didactic purpose—and this perhaps explains his love for "vile people."

If one thinks of Louisville merely as a public, there is not much of an issue here. Mr. Kopit's play is free speech, protected by the First Amendment, and that is that. If, however, one thinks of Louisville as a community or even as potentially a community, then the issue is sizable, and it is difficult. A public, as I have already suggested, is a rather odd thing; I can't think of anything else that is like it. A community is another matter, for it exists within a system of analogies or likenesses that clarify and amplify its meaning. A healthy community is like an ecosystem, and it includes—or it makes itself harmoniously a part of—its local ecosystem. It is also like a household; it is the household of its place, and it includes the households of many families, human and nonhuman. And to extend Saint Paul's famous metaphor by only a little, a healthy community is like a body, for its members mutually support and serve one another.

If a community, then, is like a household, what are we to make of the artist whose intention is to offend? Would I welcome into my house any stranger who came, proud of his bad taste, professing his love for vile people and proposing to offend almost everyone? I would not, and I do not know anybody who would. To do so would contradict self-respect and respect for loved ones. By the same token, I cannot see that a community is under any obligation to welcome such a person. The public, so far as I can see, has no right to require a community to submit to or support statements that offend it.

I know that for a century or so many artists and writers have felt it was their duty—a mark of their honesty and courage—to offend their audience. But if the artist has a duty to offend, does not the audience therefore have a duty to be offended? If the public has a duty to protect speech that is offensive to the community, does not the community have the duty to respond, to be offended, and so defend itself against the offense? A community, as a part of a public, has no right to silence publicly protected speech, but it certainly has a right not to listen and to refuse its patronage to speech that it finds offensive. It is remarkable, however, that many writers and artists appear to be unable to accept this obvious and necessary limitation on their public freedom; they seem to think that freedom entitles them not only to be offensive but also to be approved and subsidized by the people whom they have offended.

These people believe, moreover, that any community attempt to remove a book from a reading list in a public school is censorship and a violation of the freedom of speech. The situation here involves what may be a hopeless conflict of freedoms. A teacher in a public school ought to be free to exercise his or her freedom of speech in choosing what books to teach and in deciding what to say about them. (This, to my mind, would certainly include the right to teach that the Bible is the word of God and the right to teach that it is not.) But the families of a community surely must be allowed an equal freedom to determine the education of their children. How free are parents who have no choice but to turn their children over to the influence of whatever the public will prescribe or tolerate? They obviously are not free at all. The only solution is trust between a community and its teachers, who will therefore teach as members of the community—a trust that in a time of community disintegration is perhaps not possible. And so the public presses its invasion deeper and deeper into community life under the justification of a freedom far too simply understood. It is now altogether possible for a teacher who is forbidden to teach the Bible to teach some other book that is not morally acceptable to the community, perhaps in order to improve the community by shocking or offending it. It is therefore possible that the future of community life in this country may depend on private schools and home schooling.

Does my objection to the intention to offend and the idea of improvement by offense mean that I believe it is invariably wrong to offend or that I think community and public life do not need improving? Obviously not. I do not mean at all to slight the issues of honesty and of artistic integrity that are involved. But I would distinguish between the intention to offend and the willingness to risk offending. Honesty and artistic integrity do not require anyone to intend to give offense, though they certainly may cause offense. The intention to offend, it seems to me, identifies the would-be offender as a public person. I cannot imagine anyone who is a member of a community who would purposely or gladly or proudly offend it, though I know very well that honesty might require one to do so.

Here we are verging on a distinction that had better be explicitly made. There is a significant difference between works of art made to be the vital possessions of a community (existing or not) and those made merely as offerings to the public. Some artists, and I am one of them, wish to live and work within a community, or within the hope of community, in a given place. Others wish to live and work outside the claims of any community, and these now appear to be an overwhelming majority. There is a difference between these two kinds of artists but not necessarily a division. The division comes when the public art begins to conventionalize an antipathy to community life and to the moral standards that enable and protect community life, as our public art has now done. Mr. Kopit's expressed eagerness to offend a local audience he does not know is representative of this antipathy. Our public art now communicates a conventional prejudice against old people, history, parental authority, religious faith, sexual discipline, manual work, rural people and rural life, anything local or small or inexpensive. At its worst, it glamorizes or glorifies drugs, promiscuity, pornography, violence, and blasphemy. Any threat to suppress or limit these public expressions will provoke much support for the freedom of speech. I concur in this. But as a community artist, I would like to go beyond my advocacy of the freedom of speech to deplore some of the uses that are made of it, and I wish that more of my fellow artists would do so as well.

I wish that artists and all advocates and beneficiaries of the First Amendment would begin to ask, for instance, how the individual can be liberated by disobeying the moral law, when the community obviously can be liberated only by obeying it. I wish that they would consider the probability that there is a direct relation between the public antipathy to community life and local ("provincial") places and the industrial destruction of communities and places. I wish, furthermore, that they could see that artists who make offensiveness an artistic or didactic procedure are drawing on a moral capital that they may be using up. A public is shockable or offendable only to the extent that it is already un-complacent and uncorrupt—to the extent, in other words, that it is a community or remembers being one. What happens after the audience becomes used to being shocked and is therefore no longer shockable—as is apparently near to being the case with the television audience? What if offenses become stimulants—either to imitate the offenses or to avenge them? And what is the difference between the artist who wishes to offend the "provincials" and the industrialist or developer who wishes to dispossess them or convert them into a "labor force"?

The idea that people can be improved by being offended will finally have to meet the idea (espoused some of the time by some of the same people) that books, popular songs, movies, television shows, sex videos, and so on are "just fiction" or "just art" and therefore exist "for their own sake" and have no influence. To argue that works of art are "only" fictions or self-expressions and therefore cannot cause bad behavior is to argue also that they cannot cause good behavior. It is, moreover, to make an absolute division between art and life, experience and life, mind and body—a division that is intolerable to anyone who is at all serious about being a human or a member of a community or even a citizen.

Ananda Coomaraswamy, who had exhaustive knowledge of the traditional uses of art, wrote that "the purpose of any art . . . is to teach, to delight, *and above all to move*" (my emphasis).[19] Of course art moves us! To assume otherwise not only contradicts the common assumption of teachers and writers from the earliest times almost until now; it contradicts everybody's experience. A cathedral, to mention only one of the most obvious examples, is a work of art made to cause a movement toward God, and this is in part a physical movement required by the building's structure and symbolism. But all works of any power move us, in both body and mind, from the most exalted music or poetry to the simplest dance tune. In fact, a dance tune is as good an example as a cathedral. An influence is cast over us, and we are moved. If we see that the influence is bad, we may be moved to reject it, but that is a second movement; it occurs only after we have felt the power of the influence. People do not patronize the makers of pornographic films and sex videos because they are dispassionate appreciators of bad art; they do so because they wish to be moved. Perhaps the makers of pornographic films do not care what their products move their patrons to do. But if they do care, they are writing a check on moral capital to which they do not contribute. They trust that people who are moved by their work will not be moved to sexual harassment or child molestation or rape. They are banking heavily on the moral decency of their customers. And so are all of us who defend the freedom of speech. We are trusting—and not comfortably—that people who come under the influence of the sexual pandering, the greed, the commercial seductions, the moral oversimplification, the brutality, and the violence of our modern public arts will yet somehow remain under the influence of Moses and Jesus. I don't see how anyone can extend this trust without opposing in every way short of suppression the abuses and insults that are protected by it. The more a society comes to be divided in its assumptions and values, the more necessary public freedom becomes. But the more necessary public freedom becomes, the more necessary community responsibility becomes. This connection is unrelenting. And we should not forget that the finest works of art make a community of sorts of their audience. They do not divide people or justify or flatter their divisions; they define our commonwealth, and they enlarge it.

The health of a free public—especially that of a large nation under a representative government—depends on distrust. Thomas Jefferson thought so, and I believe he was right. In subscribing, generation after generation, to our Constitution, we extend to one another and to our government a trust that would be foolish if there were any better alternative. It is a breathtaking act of faith. And this trust is always so near to being misapplied that it cannot be maintained without distrust. People would fail it worse than they do if it were not for the constant vigilance and correction of distrust.

But a community makes itself up in more intimate circumstances than a public. And the health of a community depends absolutely on trust. A community knows itself and knows its place in a way that is impossible for a public (a nation, say, or a state). A community does not come together by a covenant, by a conscientious granting of trust. It exists by proximity, by neighborhood; it knows face to face, and it trusts as it knows. It learns, in the course of time and experience, what and who can be trusted. It knows that some of its members are untrustworthy, and it can be tolerant, because to know in this matter is to be safe. A community member can be trusted to be untrustworthy and so can be included. (A community can trust its liars to be liars, for example, and so enjoy them.) But if a community withholds trust, it withholds membership. If it cannot trust, it cannot exist.

One of the essential trusts of community life is that which holds marriages and families together. Another trust is that neighbors will help one another. Another is that privacy will be respected, especially the privacy of personal feeling and the privacy of relationships. All these trusts are absolutely essential, and all are somewhat fragile. But the most fragile, the most vulnerable to public invasion, is the trust that protects privacy. And in our time privacy has been the trust that has been most subjected to public invasion.

I am referring not just to the pryings and snoopings of our secret government, which contradict all that our public government claims to stand for, but also to those by now conventional publications of private grief, of violence to strangers, of the sexual coupling of strangers—all of which allow the indulgence of curiosity without sympathy. These all share in the evil of careless or malicious gossip; like careless or malicious gossip of any other kind, they destroy community by destroying respect for personal dignity and by destroying compassion. It is clear that no self-respecting human being or community would tolerate for a moment the representation of brutality or murder, on television or anywhere else, in such a way as to allow no compassion for the victim. But worst of all—and, I believe, involved in all—is the public prostitution of sex in guises of freedom ranging from the clinical to the commercial, from the artistic to the statistical.

One of the boasts of our century is that its artists— not to mention its psychologists, therapists, anthropologists, sociologists, statisticians, and pornographers

—have pried open the bedroom door at last and shown us sexual love for what it "really" is. We have, we assume, cracked the shell of sexual privacy. The resulting implication that the shell is easily cracked disguises the probability that the shell is, in fact, not crackable at all and that what we have seen displayed is not private or intimate sex, not sexual love, but sex reduced, degraded, oversimplified, and misrepresented by the very intention to display it. Sex publicly displayed is public sex. Sex observed is not private or intimate and cannot be.

Could a voyeur conceivably crack the shell? No, for voyeurs are the most handicapped of all the sexual observers; they know only what they see. True intimacy, even assuming that it can be observed, cannot be known by an outsider and cannot be shown. An artist who undertakes to show the most intimate union of lovers—even assuming that the artist is one of the lovers—can only represent what she or he alone thinks it is. The intimacy, the union itself, remains unobserved. One cannot enter into this intimacy and watch it at the same time, any more than the mind can think about itself while it thinks about something else.

Is sexual love, then, not a legitimate subject of the imagination? It is. But the work of the imagination does not require that the shell be cracked. From Homer to Shakespeare, from the Bible to Jane Austen, we have many imaginings of the intimacy and power of sexual love that have respected absolutely its essential privacy and thus have preserved its intimacy and honored its dignity.

The essential and inscrutable privacy of sexual love is the sign both of its mystery and sanctity and of its humorousness. It is mysterious because the couple who are in it are lost in it. It is their profoundest experience of the being of the world and of their being in it and is at the same time an obliviousness to the world. This lostness of people in sexual love tends to be funny to people who are outside it. But having subscribed to the superstition that we have stripped away all privacy—and mystery and sanctity—from sex, we have become oddly humorless about it. Most people, for example, no longer seem to be aware of the absurdity of sexual vanity. Most people apparently see the sexual pretension and posturing of popular singers, athletes, and movie stars as some kind of high achievement, not the laughable inanity that it really is. Sexual arrogance, on the other hand, is not funny. It is dangerous, and there are some signs that our society has begun to recognize the danger. What it has not recognized is that the publication of sexual privacy is not only fraudulent but often also a kind of sexual arrogance, and a dangerous one.

Does this danger mean that any explicit representation of sexual lovemaking is inevitably wrong? It does not. But it means that such representations *can* be wrong and that when they are wrong, they are destructive.

The danger, I would suggest, is not in the representation but in the reductiveness that is the risk of representation and that is involved in most representations. What is so fearfully arrogant and destructive is the implication that what is represented, or representable, is all there is. In the best representations, I think, there would be a stylization or incompleteness that would convey the artist's honest acknowledgment that this is not all.

The best representations are surrounded and imbued with the light of imagination, so that they make one aware, with profound sympathy, of the two lives, not just the two bodies, that are involved; they make one aware also of the difficulty of full and open sexual consent between two people and of the history and the trust that are necessary to make possible that consent. Without such history and trust, sex is brutal, no matter what species is involved.

When sexual lovemaking is shown in art, one can respond intelligently to it by means of a handful of questions: Are the lovers represented as merely "physical" bodies or as two living souls? Does the representation make it possible to see why Eros has been understood not as an instinct or a "drive" but as a god? Are we asked to see this act as existing in and of and for itself or as joined to the great cycle of fertility and mortality? Does it belong to nature and to culture? Can we imagine this sweetness continuing on through the joys and difficulties of homemaking, the births and the upbringing of children, the deaths of parents and friends—through disagreements, hardships, quarrels, aging, and death? Does it encourage us to forget or to remember that "certainly it must some time come to pass that the very gentle Beatrice will die"?[20]

And finally we must ask how the modern representations of lovemaking that we find in movies, books, paintings, sculptures, and on television measure up to the best love scenes that we know. The best love scene that I know is not explicitly sexual. It is the last scene of *The Winter's Tale*, in which Shakespeare brings onto the same stage, into the one light, young love in its astounding beauty, ardor, and hope, and old love with its mortal wrongs astoundingly graced and forgiven.

The relevance of such imagining is urgently practical; it is the propriety or justness that holds art and the world together. To represent sex without this fullness of imagination is to foreshadow the degradation and destruction of all that is not imagined. Just as the ruin of farmers, farming, and farmland may be predicted from a society's failure to imagine food in all its meanings and connections, so the failure to imagine sex in all its power and sanctity is to prepare the ruin of family and community life and of much else. In order to expose the privacy of sex, we have made of it another industrial specialization, leaving it naked not only of clothes and of customary discretions and courtesies but also of all its cultural and natural connections.

There are, we must realize, kinds of nakedness that are significantly and sometimes ominously different from each other. To know this, we have only to study the examples that are before us. There is—and who can ever forget it?—the nakedness of the photographs of prisoners in Hitler's death camps. This is the nakedness of absolute exposure to mechanical politics, politics gravitating toward the unimagining "efficiency" of machinery. I remember also a photograph of a naked small child running terrified down a dirt road in Vietnam, showing the body's absolute exposure to the indifference of air war, the appropriate technology of mechanical politics.

There is also the nakedness in advertising, in the worst kinds of fashionable or commercial art. This is the nakedness of free-market sexuality, the nakedness that is possible only in a society in which price is the only index of worth.

The nakedness of the death camps and of mechanical war denotes an absolute loss of dignity. In advertising, novels, and movies, the nakedness sometimes denotes a very significant and a very dangerous loss of dignity. Where the body has no dignity, where the sanctity of its own mystery and privacy is not recognized by a surrounding and protecting community, there can be no freedom. To destroy the dignity of the body—the dignity of any and every body—is to prepare the way for the enslaver, the rapist, the torturer, the user of cannon fodder. The nakedness or near-nakedness of some tribal peoples (I judge from the photographs that I have seen) is, in contrast, always dignified, and this dignity rests on a trust so complex and comprehensive as to be virtually unimaginable to us. The public nakedness of our own society involves no trust but only an exploitiveness that is inescapably economic and greedy. It is an abandonment of the self to self-exploitation and to exploitation by others.

There is also the nakedness of innocence, as, for example, in Degas's *Seated Bather Drying Herself*, in the Metropolitan Museum of Art, in which the body is shown in the unaware and unregarded coherence and mystery of its own being. This quality D. H. Lawrence saw and celebrated:

> *People were bathing and posturing themselves on the beach
> and all was dreary, great robot limbs, robot breasts
> robot voices, robot even the gay umbrellas.
> But a woman, shy and alone, was washing herself under
> a tap
> and the glimmer of the presence of the gods was like lilies
> and like water-lilies.*[21]

Finally, there is the nakedness of sexual candor. However easy or casual nakedness may have been made by public freedom, the nakedness of sexual candor is not possible except within the culturally delineated conditions that establish and maintain trust. And it is utterly private. It can be suggested in art but not represented. Any effort to represent it, I suspect, will inevitably be bogus. What must we do to earn the freedom of being unguardedly and innocently naked to someone? Our own and other cultures suggest that we must do a lot. We must make promises and keep them. We must assume many fearful responsibilities and do much work. We must build the household of trust.

It is the community, not the public, that is the protector of the possibility of this candor, just as it is the protector of other tender, vulnerable, and precious things—the childhood of children, for example, and the fertility of fields. These protections are left to the community, for they can be protected only by affection and by intimate knowledge, which are beyond the capacities of the public and beyond the power of the private citizen.

IV

If the word *community* is to mean or amount to anything, it must refer to a place (in its natural integrity) and its people. It must refer to a placed people. Since there obviously can be no cultural relationship that is uniform between a nation and a continent, "community" must mean a people locally placed and a people, moreover, not too numerous to have a common knowledge of themselves and of their place. Because places differ from one another and because people will differ somewhat according to the characters of their places, if we think of a nation as an assemblage of many communities, we are necessarily thinking of some sort of pluralism.

There is, in fact, a good deal of talk about pluralism

these days, but most of it that I have seen is fashionable, superficial, and virtually worthless. It does not foresee or advocate a plurality of settled communities but is only a sort of indifferent charity toward a plurality of aggrieved groups and individuals. It attempts to deal liberally—that is, by the superficial courtesies of tolerance and egalitarianism—with a confusion of claims.

The social and cultural pluralism that some now see as a goal is a public of destroyed communities. Wherever it exists, it is the result of centuries of imperialism. The modern industrial urban centers are "pluralistic" because they are full of refugees from destroyed communities, destroyed community economies, disintegrated local cultures, and ruined local ecosystems. The pluralists who see this state of affairs as some sort of improvement or as the beginning of "global culture" are being historically perverse, as well as politically naive. They wish to regard liberally and tolerantly the diverse, sometimes competing claims and complaints of a rootless society, and yet they continue to tolerate also the ideals and goals of the industrialism that caused the uprooting. They affirm the pluralism of a society formed by the uprooting of cultures at the same time that they regard the fierce self-defense of still-rooted cultures as "fundamentalism," for which they have no tolerance at all. They look with wistful indulgence and envy at the ruined or damaged American Indian cultures so long as those cultures remain passively a part of our plurality, forgetting that these cultures, too, were once "fundamentalist" in their self-defense. And when these cultures again attempt self-defense—when they again assert the inseparability of culture and place—they are opposed by this pluralistic society as self-righteously as ever. The tolerance of this sort of pluralism extends always to the uprooted and passive, never to the rooted and active.

The trouble with the various movements of rights and liberties that have passed among us in the last thirty years is that they have all been too exclusive and so have degenerated too readily into special pleading. They have, separately, asked us to stop exploiting racial minorities or women or nature, and they have been, separately, right to do so. But they have not, separately or together, come to the realization that we live in a society that exploits, first, everything that is not ourselves and then, inevitably, ourselves. To ask, within this general onslaught, that we should honor the dignity of this or that group is to ask that we should swim up a waterfall.

Any group that takes itself, its culture, and its values seriously enough to try to separate, or to remain separate, from the industrial line of march will be, to say the least, unwelcome in the plurality. The tolerance of these doctrinaire pluralists always runs aground on religion. You may be fascinated by religion, you may study it, anthropologize and psychoanalyze about it, collect and catalogue its artifacts, but you had better not believe in it. You may put into "the canon" the holy books of any group, but you had better not think them holy. The shallowness and hypocrisy of this tolerance is exposed by its utter failure to extend itself to the suffering people of Iraq, who are, by the standards of this tolerance, fundamentalist, backward, unprogressive, and in general not like "us."

The problem with this form of pluralism is that it has no authentic standard; its standard simply is what one group or another may want at the moment. Its professed freedom is not that of community life but rather that of a political group acting on the pattern of individualism. To get farther toward a practicable freedom, the group must measure itself and its wants by standards external to itself. I assume that these standards must be both cultural and ecological. If people wish to be free, then they must preserve the culture that makes for political freedom, and they must preserve the health of the world.

There is an insistently practical question that any person and any group seriously interested in freedom must ask: Can land and people be preserved anywhere by means of a culture that is in the usual sense pluralistic? E. M. Forster, writing *Howards End* in the first decade of this century, doubted that they could. Nothing that has happened in the intervening eighty-odd years diminishes that doubt, and much that has happened confirms it.

A culture capable of preserving land and people can be made only within a relatively stable and enduring relationship between a local people and its place. Community cultures made in this way would necessarily differ, and sometimes radically so, from one place to another, because places differ. This is the true and necessary pluralism. There can, I think, be no national policy of pluralism or multiculturalism but only these pluralities of local cultures. And if these cultures are of any value and worthy of any respect, they will not be elective—not determined by mere wishes—but will be formed in response to local nature and local needs.

At present, the rhetoric of racial and cultural pluralism works against the possibility of a pluralism of settled communities, exactly as do the assumptions and the practices of national and global economies. So long as we try to think of ourselves as African Americans or

European Americans or Asian Americans, we will never settle anywhere. For an authentic community is made less in reference to who we are than to where we are. I cannot farm my farm as a European American—or as an American, or as a Kentuckian—but only as a person belonging to the place itself. If I am to use it well and live on it authentically, I cannot do so by knowing where my ancestors came from (which, except for one great-grandfather, I do not know and probably can never know); I can do so only by knowing where I am, what the nature of the place permits me to do here, and who and what are here with me. To know these things, I must ask the place. A knowledge of foreign cultures is useful, perhaps indispensable, to me in my effort to settle here, but it cannot tell me where I am.

That there should be peace, commerce, and biological and cultural outcrosses among local cultures is obviously desirable and probably necessary as well. But such a state of things would be radically unlike what is now called pluralism. To start with, a plurality of settled communities could not be preserved by the present-day pluralists' easy assumption that all cultures are equal or of equal value and capable of surviving together by tolerance. The idea of equality is a good one, so long as it means "equality before the law." Beyond that, the idea becomes squishy and sentimental because of manifest inequalities of all kinds. It makes no sense, for example, to equate equality with freedom. The two concepts must be joined precisely and within strict limits if their association is to make any sense at all. Equality, in certain circumstances, is anything but free. If we have equality and nothing else—no compassion, no magnanimity, no courtesy, no sense of mutual obligation and dependence, no imagination—then power and wealth will have their way; brutality will rule. A general and indiscriminate egalitarianism is free-market culture, which, like free-market economics, tends toward a general and destructive uniformity. And tolerance, in association with such egalitarianism, is a way of ignoring the reality of significant differences. If I merely tolerate my neighbors on the assumption that all of us are equal, that means I can take no interest in the question of which ones of us are right and which ones are wrong; it means that I am denying the community the use of my intelligence and judgment; it means that I am not prepared to defer to those whose abilities are superior to mine, or to help those whose condition is worse; it means that I can be as self-centered as I please.

In order to survive, a plurality of true communities would require not egalitarianism and tolerance but knowledge, an understanding of the necessity of local differences, and respect. Respect, I think, always implies imagination—the ability to see one another, across our inevitable differences, as living souls.

NOTES

Chapter 7: Christianity and the Survival of Creation

1. Psalms 24:1. (All biblical quotations are from the King James Version.)
2. Leviticus 25:23.
3. John 1:3.
4. Job 34:14–15.
5. Philip Sherrard, *Human Image: World Image* (Ipswich, Suffolk, England: Golgonooza Press, 1992), 152.
6. George Herbert, "Providence," lines 41 and 44, from *The Poems of George Herbert*, ed. by Helen Gardner (London: Oxford University Press, 1961), 54.
7. Dante Alighieri, *The Divine Comedy*, trans. by Charles S. Singleton, Bollingen Series LXXX, and *Inferno*, canto XI, lines 46–48 (Princeton, NJ: Princeton University Press, 1970).
8. Dante Alighieri, *Inferno*, canto XI, lines 109–11.
9. William Blake, *Complete Writings*, ed. by Geoffrey Keynes (London: Oxford University Press, 1966), 160.
10. Kathleen Raine, *Golgonooza: City of Imagination* (Ipswich, Suffolk, England: Golgonooza Press, 1991), 28.
11. 1 Kings 8:27.
12. Acts 17:24 and 28.
13. Matthew 18:20.
14. Isaiah 1:13–17.
15. Romans 1:20.
16. Deuteronomy 33:13–16.
17. Matthew 16:26.
18. William Shakespeare, *Macbeth*, ed. by Kenneth Muir (Cambridge, MA: Harvard University Press, 1957), V,v, lines 13, 26–28, 49.

19. Ananda K. Coomaraswamy, *Christian and Oriental Philosophy of Art* (New York: Dover, 1957), 98.
20. Walter Shewring, *Artist and Tradesman* (Marlborough, MA: Paulinus Press, 1984), 19.
21. Herbert, *The Poems of George Herbert*, 54.
22. June Sprigg, *By Shaker Hands* (Hanover, NH: University Press of New England, 1990), 33.
23. Ananda K. Coomaraswamy, *Selected Papers*, vol. 1 (Princeton, NJ: Princeton University Press, 1977), 255, 259.
24. Coomaraswamy, *Christian and Oriental Philosophy of Art*, 99.
25. Dante, *Paradiso*, canto XIII, lines 121 and 123.
26. Mark Twain, *Adventures of Huckleberry Finn*, in *Mississippi Writings* (New York: Library of America, 1982), 626.
27. Matthew 5:44.
28. George MacDonald, *A Time for Trumpets* (New York: Bantam Books, 1984), 458.

Chapter 8: Sex, Economy, Freedom, and Community

1. E. M. Forster, *Howards End* (New York: Vintage, 1989), 304.
2. Henry Swainson Cowper, *Hawkshead (The Northernmost Parish of Lancashire): Its History, Archaeology, Industries, Dialect, Etc.* (London: Bemrose & Sons, 1899), 209.
3. Harry M. Caudill, *Theirs Be the Power* (Urbana and Chicago: University of Illinois Press, 1983).
4. Helena Norberg-Hodge, *Ancient Futures: Learning from Ladakh* (San Francisco: Sierra Club Books, 1991), 101–102.
5. Ibid., 146.
6. Humphrey Jennings, *Pandaemonium, 1660–1886: The Coming of the Machine as Seen by Contemporary Observers* (New York: Free Press, 1985), 131–32.
7. *Encyclopaedia Britannica*, 14th ed., S.V., "Luddite."
8. Psalms 139:14.
9. John Donne, *The Songs and Sonnets of John Donne*, 2nd ed., ed. by Theodore Redpath (New York: St. Martin's Press, 1983), 218–20.
10. Wallace Stevens, *The Collected Poems* (New York: Alfred A. Knopf, 1955), 17.

11. Dante, *La Vita Nuova*, trans. by D. G. Rossetti, XIV, in *The Portable Dante*, ed. by Paolo Milano (New York: Viking, 1967), 566.

12. *The Way of Life According to Lao-tzu*, trans. by Witter Bynner (New York: Capricorn Books, 1962), 49.

13. John 8:32.

14. Thomas Jefferson, *Writings* (New York: Library of America, 1984), 493.

15. Mary McGrory, "Ed Meese on the Stand," Louisville, KY, *Courier-Journal* (March 31, 1989).

16. Judith Weissman, *Half Savage and Hardy and Free: Women and Rural Radicalism in the Nineteenth-Century Novel* (Middletown, CT: Wesleyan University Press, 1987). See especially the introduction and chapter 1.

17. Ibid., 31.

18. Louisville, KY, *Courier-Journal* (Feb. 26, 1989), Section I, p. 1.

19. Coomaraswamy, *Selected Papers*, vol. II (Princeton, NJ: Princeton University Press, 1977), 37.

20. Dante, *La Vita Nuova*, XXIII.

21. D. H. Lawrence, "The Gods! The Gods!," *Collected Poems*, vol. 2, ed. by Vivian de Sola Pinto and Warren Roberts (New York: Viking, 1964), 651.

A native Kentuckian, Wendell Berry lived and taught in New York and California before returning permanently to the Kentucky River region. For the last three decades he has lived and farmed with his family on a small farm in Henry County. He is a past fellow of both the Guggenheim Foundation and the Rockefeller Foundation, and was a Stegner Fellow at Stanford University. He has received, among other awards, the Victory of Spirit Ethics Award in 1992 from the Louisville Community Foundation and the University of Louisville, and the Lannan Foundation Award for Nonfiction in 1989.

Berry is the author of more than two dozen books of fiction, poetry, and essays, including *What Are People For?*, *The Gift of Good Land*, and *Home Economics*. Currently he lives and writes on his farm in Kentucky and teaches at the University of Kentucky.